THE ORIGINAL VISION

THE ORIGINAL VISION

A Study of the Religious Experience of Childhood

EDWARD ROBINSON

Introduction by
John H. Westerhoff, III

The Seabury Press / New York

1983
The Seabury Press
815 Second Avenue
New York, N.Y. 10017

Printed in the United States of America

ISBN 0-8164-2439-X

We are grateful to the Hibbert Trust for their support and encouragement, and
in particular for a generous grant towards the costs of publication.

We gratefully acknowledge permission from the following to quote copyright
material:
Editions Aubier Montaigne, Gabriel Marcel, *Homo Viator;* Chatto and Win-
dus, Ltd., Edwin Muir, *Autobiography;* Dover Publications, Inc., Otto Rank,
Beyond Psychology; Editions Gallimard, André Malraux, *Antimemoirs;* The
Hogarth Press, Erik Erikson, *Childhood and Society,* and *The Standard
Edition of the Complete Psychological Works of Sigmund Freud,* tr. and ed.
by James Strachey, vol. XXI; Dr. Peter Lomas, *True and False Experience;*
Methuen and Co., Ltd., Liam Hudson, *Contrary Imaginations;* Oxford Uni-
versity Press, John Bowker, *The Sense of God;* Penguin Books, Ltd., Sylvia
Anthony, *The Discovery of Death in Childhood and After;* Routledge and
Kegan Paul, Ltd., J. Piaget, *The Child's Conception of the World,* J. Piaget
and B. Inhelder, *The Psychology of the Child,* and J. W. Tibble (ed.), *The
Study of Education.*

A child has a picture of human existence peculiar to himself, which he probably never remembers after he has lost it: the original vision of the world. I think of this picture or vision as that of a state in which the earth, the houses on the earth, and the life of every human being are related to the sky overarching them; as if the sky fitted the earth and the earth the sky. Certain dreams convince me that a child has this vision, in which there is a completer harmony of all things with each other than he will ever know again.

Edwin Muir

CONTENTS

INTRODUCTION TO THE AMERICAN EDITION

You are about to read a rare book. If you care about religious education it may be among the most important you will ever read. I am aware that this is a phenomenal claim. Ever so infrequently, a book appears that not only has some unique contemporary relevance, but possible lasting significance. This is just such a book.

Five years ago, Maria Harris—Professor of Religious Education at Andover Newton Theological Seminary, my colleague, friend, and book editor for the journal *Religious Education*—introduced me to Edward Robinson's *The Original Vision*. I have been quoting it and assigning it to my classes at Duke ever since. It has been extremely difficult, however, to acquire copies in the United States, for it—along with *The Images of Life* and *Knowing and Unknowing* by Brenda Lealman (Robinson's colleague) and Edward Robinson—was originally published in England. Now, thanks to The Seabury Press, this significant work will be able to receive the broad readership that it deserves in this country.

Perhaps a few words of background will be helpful. In 1963, Sir Alister Hardy, the renowned British scientist, challenged his fellow scientists in his Gifford Lectures to take seriously the fact of religious experience as a central feature of human life. Rising to his own challenge, in 1969 he founded the Religious Experience Research Unit at Manchester College, Oxford. A decade later he published *The Spiritual Nature of Man,* the most seminal analysis of the phenomena of religious experience since that of another Gifford Lecturer, William James. Now in this volume, the Unit's new director, Edward Robinson, reports on the religious experience of childhood. Few existing books offer greater insights for understanding religious life and spiritual awareness or suggest greater consequences for shaping a theory of religious education than this.

Permit me, in this short introduction, to suggest a few reasons for this contention, along with a few preliminary implications as a personal statement intended to stimulate you to explore Robinson's findings yourself and thereby draw your own conclusions.

First, as to method. For much too long the methodology of experimental psychology has dominated our study of human nature. This work provides us, at long last, with a renewed effort to use the methodology of cultural anthropology (participant-observation, in this case in the form of biographical notes and case histories). Insofar as research findings are limited and influenced by our methods of investigation, the methods best suited to the phenomenon under study are necessary. No single method can be acceptable. While not as precise as that used by experimental psychology, the methodology of cultural anthropology is particularly appropriate to both the study of religion and the religious.

Second, Robinson suggests a useful and I believe necessary alternative theory to developmentalism with its concerns for predictability, universality, and control. As Dorothee Sölle, the German theologian, once commented: "In a time when learning theories tend more and more to be reduced to a technical model within the framework of which the conditions under which we can learn and experience are researched and put into operation, we need a counter model." Now we have one. While Freudianism and Behaviorism (Skinner *et al.*) still influence many, developmentalism (Piaget, Kohlberg, and Fowler) has become the dominant school of thought underlying contemporary religious education theory. While insights from these theories continue to have value and relevance, they are not exhaustive and should not be assumed to be so. More important, they are limited by their presuppositions; every theory is. Religious experience, for example, is always personal and hence particular; it is rarely predictable and surely never controllable.

Further, the observation of children used by developmentalists may not be the best way to develop a theory for understanding the religious experience of children. Indeed, childhood may be best understood as a dimension of life (not a chronological period) about which we can only become fully conscious in later life through an exploration of childhood memories, a suggestion of particular significance in shaping a theory of religious experience during childhood. For example, religious experience may be complete and full during childhood, an element of the whole person which can be nurtured, lost for a time, rediscovered, suppressed, crippled, or atrophied in later life. Childhood may reveal to us one significant and unique way of knowing and of knowledge, which—while fundamental to the childhood years—is also essential to later conceptualizations and understandings. Developmentalism, regrettably, begins with the assumption that children are incapable of experiencing, perceiving, or thinking as mature adults. A child's way is considered inadequate and underdeveloped. The developmentalist aim, therefore, is to discover how children develop mature, adult ways of experiencing, perceiving, and thinking so that we might assist or influence their progressive movement through stages of lesser to higher means.

Robinson, on the other hand, assumes that children have a natural capacity for insight, imagination, understanding, and knowing that does not need to develop into some higher form. Chidren, he found, have experiences that are essentially religious; and he further found that no mature religious life is possible without the presence and continuance of such experiences.

Gabriel Moran, the Roman Catholic religious educator, in his seminal work *Education Toward Adulthood,* makes the point that we have set adult learning and education over against childhood learning and education. Children, he observed, are typically described as non-rational, non-productive, and dependent; adults as rational, productive and independent. Since children do not think intellectually (abstractly), they do not think; since they do not know rationally, they do not know. Their subjective experiences and intuitive ways of knowing are depreciated, their ability to perceive or understand the real world is questioned. But, as he wisely comments, maturity is the integration of these polar opposites. To be mature is to have fully integrated our non-rational (intuitive) and rational (intellectual) capacities, our non-productive (contemplative) and productive (active) natures, our dependent and independent modes of behavior, into interdependency.

Third, for too long religious education, following the lead of general education, has focused on cognition, objective reflection, and decision making (all appropriate and reasonable for adults), thereby depreciating the nurturing of the imagination and the affections and the use of the arts (all appropriate and natural for children) in the educational process. The findings of Robinson, it seems to me, provide us with a defensible alternative for religious education with all ages, but especially with children; an alternative that is not just a set of activities for use with children until they grow up, but ones which are essential to the religious life.

The arts incarnate our experience of mystery, wonder, and awe; they thereby aid us to encounter the holy or sacred. A number of years ago the College Society for Church Work held a symposium of poets and theologians at the College of Preachers in Washington, D.C. In the first conversations over the papers prepared for the gathering, Denise Levertov, a poet, commented that it seemed in a peculiar way that the poets were the believers and the theologians the skeptics. "God speaks," writes Frederick Buechner in his biographical work *The Sacred Journey;* "the reason that his words are impossible to capture in human language is, of course, that they are ultimately always incarnate words. They are words fleshed out in the everydayness, no less than the crises of our human experience." He then explains that he started to write poetry because he had had enough of the surface of life and was suddenly drawn to what had always lain beneath the surface, inside himself and his earliest life experiences.

Our knowledge of God is prior to our conceptualizations of God. Religious thought is grounded in religious experiences. Our personal encounter with that ultimate mystery which is God is nurtured, expressed, and communicated through dance, music, drama, poetry, painting, sculpture, and film, through the stimulation of the imagination and our visual, oral, and kinetic senses. Religious experience and the arts are related; so are religious experience and liturgy. Through ritual, repetitive symbolic aesthetic actions expressive of the community's story (memory and vision) and liturgy's contact with our subjective, experiental, intuitive modes of consciousness (modes natural to childhood), the religious imagination and the religious affections are enhanced and enlivened. The distance we have put between ourselves (especially children), the arts, and liturgy have impoverished our religious experience and diminished the effectiveness of educational ministries.

For me, at least, the implications are clear. Children can and do have profound, mature religious experiences which only in later life can be named, described, explained, or comprehended. These religious experiences are related to or at least nurtured and stimulated by the aesthetic as it is participated in and expressed through the arts and liturgy. We know about religion before we know what religion is about. Religious awareness, the religious imagination, the experience of the holy or sacred, is natural to childhood. Just as religion is danced before it is believed, it is experienced before it is explained; we hear God speak before we can express what God says. The aims of religious education should encompass religious awareness and experience. Children, therefore, I contend, belong at the Sunday Eucharist; they need to participate in the Lord's Supper each week from the day of their baptism; they should be provided with opportunities to have their imaginations enhanced and they should be encouraged to participate in the arts. Children should be affirmed as persons who can and do have significant experiences of the divine which, while only recollected and described later in life, are still mature, mystical, numinous experiences of the holy.

If we were to take seriously the findings in this book, I believe it would revolutionize religious education. Regrettably, too many of our educational programs in local congregations work against that "original vision" which is natural to childhood and the birthright of every child. Perhaps after reading this book more adults will become aware of their own "original vision" and hence be converted in their understandings of childhood religious education. I hope so, and therefore I recommend without reservation, indeed with enthusiasm, this amazing and profound book to all those persons in the church who care about religious experience, children, and religious education.

(The Rev. Dr.) John H. Westerhoff
Professor of Religious Education
Duke University Divinity School

THE ORIGINAL VISION

FOREWORD

On the few occasions on which I have accepted an invitation to write a foreword to a book I have said that as a rule I regard such an introduction by some one other than the author as superfluous unless there is some very good reason for it. In this instance there are two such reasons.

The first is that I can say something that I feel must be said, but which the author himself, in his modesty, cannot say directly, although it will be found abundantly evident in his book by all those who read it. Partly as a result of his research and the help given to it by members of the general public and partly, indeed essentially, by his own intuitive feeling for the subject, Edward Robinson is here making a contribution of paramount importance to our understanding of childhood; this must consequently be of the highest value to all those engaged in education. It is especially significant for those who may be concerned with an approach to religious awareness and yet who, for various reasons, may have found the subject, particularly in our now pluralist or largely secular society, one that is far from easy to present with the sincerity that is essential to convincing teaching.

This book provides the material for making the spiritual side of man as real and as vital as are the facts shown in nature study to the youngest children or as, later on, the marvels of molecular biology taught in the sixth forms. It does not deal with the religion of institutions or of theologies, but with a fundamental part of man's nature, which is especially revealed in the imaginative vision of the young.

Before proceeding, as I shall in a moment, to say more about the nature of this book, I should briefly mention the second reason for my agreeing to provide a foreword. Edward Robinson kindly wished me to write it as Founder and the first

Director of our Religious Experience Research Unit in which his study was made; it is well that I should briefly place his work in relation to the wide range of research being continued now under his Directorship at the Unit and in association wth other institutions. Apart from progress reports and numerous articles, and my own more general book *The Biology of God* which discusses the philosophy behind our venture, Robinson's *The Original Vision* is the first detailed study to come from the research; it is the beginning, I hope, of a series of volumes which will deal with various aspects of the many different kinds of religious experience or spiritual awareness — call them what you will — which we are studying from first hand accounts. Our collection now consists of over 4,000 such records and is continually being added to. We are essentially playing the part of naturalists hunting specimens of human experience.

Our methods could have, I believe, a not inconsiderable bearing on the handling of religious education in our schools, so it may be well very briefly to say why I think so. We are humbly following in the footsteps of those two American pioneers who at the turn of the century were the first to make a systematic psychological study of religious experience: William James and Edwin Starbuck. Until quite recently their methods have not been followed except by the social anthropologists; we now know much more about the religious feelings of Polynesians, North American Indians and various tribes in Africa than we do about those of our fellow members of western civilization. I have said we are playing the part of naturalists; I might just as well have said we are acting as anthropologists in our own society — indeed, of course, the anthropologists *are* the naturalists of mankind. We must not allow the triumphs of experimental science to cause us to despise observational natural history. It is well to remind our pupils that the greatest contribution yet made by the study of life to the philosophy of man came not from the biological laboratories but from the work of the great field naturalists of the last century; I am referring, of course, to the concept of evolution. Darwin's theory of natural selection was based upon his careful observations of nature and those of Wallace, Bates and many others; it has since been refined, added to and converted into a quantitative science by the rediscovery of Mendel's Laws and the remarkable revelation of the molecular nature of the genetic code.

What is important to stress in schools today is that the discussion of religious feelings — I use these words rather than "religion" — is no longer to be dominated by conventional ideas of what constitutes religion, or by theological orthodoxies of one kind or another; it must be based on observational study. This is indeed as important and vital a subject to be dealt with at school as is the appreciation of art, music or natural beauty. Edward Robinson's book, I venture to prophesy, will be a powerful element in the revolution in religious studies which indeed is already under way.

"What I have called 'the original vision' of childhood", says Robinson, "is no mere imaginative fancy but a form of *knowledge* and one that is essential to the development of any mature understanding". After a brief summary of the main points of his argument he concludes: "And I believe finally that this vision and the experiences which are associated with it are essentially *religious*, and that no understanding, let alone definition, of that word is possible without a sympathetic insight into all that is here included in the concept of childhood".

He is, all the way through, presenting us with not only the evidence for the reality of this original vision but the supreme importance of keeping this divine flame burning throughout one's life. It is a flame so easily extinguished in the process of growing up; it is of cardinal importance that our system of education should be aimed at keeping it alive to endow the later man, or woman, with the imaginative spirit and enthusiasm (*en theos* — the god within!) that leads to those adventures in discovery, science, art and, yes, in religion, that mark the youthful spirit which may indeed be carried into old age.

For those who are followers of the gospels the truth of this will come home to them; I refer of course to the authorised version of Mark 10:15: "Whosoever shall not receive the kingdom of God as a little child, he shall not enter therein". The very first poem I was given to learn as a child was that by Hood called "Past and Present" which began: "I remember, I remember, the house where I was born". How I loved it, especially,

> The lilacs where the robin built,
>   And where my brother set
> The laburnum on his birthday;
>   The tree is living yet.

The last verse however I did not understand till I was much older:

> I remember, I remember
>   The fir trees dark and high;
> I used to think their slender tops
>   Were close against the sky;
> It was a childish ignorance,
>   But now 'tis little joy
> To know I'm farther off from Heaven
>   Than when I was a boy.

I may well be laughed at for quoting this little verse; I can only offer as an excuse that it is the child within me! What Hood felt was felt by Wordsworth too, but is this loss inevitable? I think not; I believe, as I have said, that the most important task for education is not only to preserve this original vision, but to see that it develops — indeed that it may be set upon a course of growth continuing after schooldays to enrich ever more fully the whole of life. This is the vital message, the challenge, of this book.

ALISTER HARDY

1

WHAT IS CHILDHOOD?

There are all sorts of ways of studying childhood.

There is, for a start, a vast literature on the subject. Child psychology has in the last half-century developed into a science of its own. The performance of children in all kinds of circumstances has been observed by experts under controlled conditions. The result has been the accumulation of a mass of information which nobody concerned with children can ignore.

Or you can do the observation for yourself. It is often a relief to turn from books on child development, not all of which can compare in liveliness with the little people they are written about, to spend an hour or two with children themselves. The weight of so much learning may seem comically disproportionate to the subject matter. Perhaps it might even be better to start without too many theoretical presuppositions. "Human beings, it seems are multifarious", observes Liam Hudson, "and we achieve little by speculating about them without first finding out what they are like."[1] Fine; but one does not have to study psychology to know that we all start with presuppositions (others with prejudices) of one kind or another; and it does no harm to discover what these are. And this is particularly true of childhood. Why is this?

There is something peculiar about childhood that makes it difficult for anyone to think straight about it. We have all of course been children once, and that alone is enough to stock us with a powerful set of presuppositions, to make us all feel we know something about the subject. But what I mean is slightly different. In most of us, in all I would hope who are reading this book, there is still some childhood left.[2]

"Quand nous ne sommes plus enfants", said Brancusi, "nous sommes déjà morts". When we are no longer children, we are already dead.[3] Childhood, as I conceive it in this book, is not just a chronological period, a developmental stage to be defined however roughly in years, separating infancy and adolescence, it is an element of the whole person. It may temporarily disappear with the onset of puberty; it may be suppressed, crippled or almost totally atrophied in later life. "If the boy within us ceases to speak to the man who enfolds him, the shape of life is broken." So writes Sean O'Faolain at the end of his autobiography. On the other hand this childhood may continue to grow and develop with life. Strictly speaking, the years between, say, 3 and 11 are the proper time for childhood, when it has most scope to establish itself. If it does not succeed then, it may have a hard time of it later on. Seen like this, childhood cannot be fully understood simply by the observation of children. Quite apart from the difficulties of communication in the pre-adolescent years, there is often a dimension to our early experiences that we can only become fully conscious of (if at all) in later life, when we compare them with other forms of experience that lack that dimension; in childhood we may be wiser than we know.

I said just now that my interest was not confined to the actual experiences of the early years. This was not always so. Before coming to join Sir Alister Hardy at the Religious Experience Research Unit at Manchester College, Oxford, I was much involved with students in training to be teachers. In this field Piaget was the dominating influence. The developmental psychology associated with his name still holds an unassailable position in western educational theory. Unassailable, because of two things. Firstly, his method is convincing; in all his studies the conclusions follow from the experimental work. Subsequent inquiries may have suggested modifications here and there, but in general the structure is sound. Secondly, his ideas about what it is important to understand about children are entirely in tune with the educational presuppositions of our society. For a culture increasingly concerned with the control of its environment and permeated with the spirit of competitive individualism, nothing could have been more timely or more appropriate than Piaget's discoveries in the field of cognitive development. The list of his titles is very impressive, and it might at first seem that there are few aspects of childhood that he has not surveyed. Many of his observations are in fact both true and valuable, and nothing that I have to say about him will I hope suggest that he was not an acute and original thinker. Nevertheless I believe that Piaget's view of childhood was a limited one, and that these limitations can have a seriously damaging or at least impoverishing effect on our educational practice. Here is a typical passage.

> Representative intelligence begins with the child's systematic concentration on his own action and on the momentary figurative aspects of the segments of reality with which this action deals. Later it arrives at a decentering based on the general co-ordination of action, and this permits the formation of operatory systems of transformations or constants or conservations which liberate the representation of reality from its deceptive figurative appearances.[4]

The starting point of all Piaget's thought about childhood is the incapacity of children to see the world as adults see it. Here, for example, he is concerned with the liberation of the mind of the child from an illusory view of reality. Reality? Piaget is a philosopher, and philosophers do not speak lightly of appearance and reality. But here as elsewhere he seems always to assume that reality is the way adults see it, and that if children do not see it that way they are victims of "deceptive figurative appearances". Where in fact there is a difference of opinion, adults are right and children wrong. Of course, under proper adult influence, children get better all the time, but this development is best measured in their relative incapacity to see this adult "reality". This approach is well illustrated in his technique of questioning. What questions, he asks, is one to put to children?

> The criterion will be as usual only to ask questions to which older children can give a correct solution, and to which the youngest

9

will give answers that improve progressively with age.[5]
"As usual": this is his regular practice.

This view of a progressive development from childhood incompetence to the adult ability to give correct solutions is reflected in, perhaps it is derived from, the prime importance given by Piaget to verbal understanding. "For a child to think", he declares, "is to deal in words."[6] A remarkable statement: does he mean to imply that children are different from adults in this respect? It is in fact this insistence on verbal criteria of development that makes Piaget's work so important to the teaching profession, and of rather less value to anyone who believes that there are positive qualities in childhood that remain undetected by such methods, slipping like water through the finest net. Piaget is in fact continually setting children an exam in a subject that adults are good at and children bad. Predictably, the children fail. If I were to write a history of music of the last four centuries, and base my judgements purely on each composer's skill in orchestration, Mendelssohn would inevitably come out better than Monteverdi, and Mahler perhaps above both. Piaget's services to educational theory have of course been great. Not only has he laid the basis for a new professionalism — how for example would one set an exam in educational psychology without having such a categorical system to base it on? There would be no correct answers — but for a society that sees its children as a resource to be developed[7] he has provided the techniques for doing this in the quickest and most efficient way. If children are really to be thought of as little more than inefficient adults, then the prime function of education is to turn them into efficient ones. Some of us may now be having our doubts about the uses to which his discoveries are sometimes put. There is something very disturbing, for example, in what Michael Frayn has called the "Grow Older Younger" school of thought: some of these experiments amount to little more than a conspiracy to rob children of their childhood, without any consideration of what may be the longer-term consequences.[8] Another misfortune has been the emergence of a concept of intelligence as something measurable in isolation from the circumstances in which it is used. Piaget cannot be held directly responsible for all these developments; yet it was an application of his principles that, for example, led Ronald Goldman to conclude that "religious insight generally begins to appear between the ages of 12 and 13".[9]

This is still accepted as orthodoxy in many quarters; there has been little fundamental change in recent years. The picture of childhood that emerges is a largely negative, not to say a patronizing one. So it was with considerable excitement that on joining this research project I found myself reading this sort of thing: "The most profound experience of my life came to me when I was very young, between 4 and 5 years old." "I just know that the whole of my life has been built on the great truth that was revealed to me then" (at the age of 6). "As far back as I can remember I have never had a sense of separation from the spiritual force I now choose to call God." This material had been sent in response to the original appeal made by Sir Alister Hardy, founder of this Research Unit. He invited all those who "felt that their lives had in any way been affected by some power beyond themselves" to write an account of the experience and the effect it had had on their lives. No mention was made of childhood; nevertheless some 15% of all our correspondents (they now number over 4,000) started by going back to events and experiences of their earliest years. Reading these accounts I began to wonder whether there were not in quite young children capacities for insight and understanding that had been underrated by the development psychologists. Here it seemed might be a valuable source of information to complement the prevailing view. My concern was still, at that stage, with childhood in the chronological sense; it was to learn more about how children think and feel, how they experience the world.

I still believe that this is an important objective, and that a study of this material can bring us nearer to it. But it is a common experience in all research, particularly in a field as little explored as this, to discover as one goes on that the questions one is asking are not the right ones. This can be very tiresome. "All my discoveries were disappointments at the time." This was said to me by a very distinguished scientist; he was emphasizing the need for a flexibility of approach, even a readiness to abandon an

11

original objective if more important possibilities emerge. So here. Consider the following account.

When I was about five I had the experience on which, in a sense, my life has been based. It has always remained real and true for me. Sitting in the garden one day I suddenly became conscious of a colony of ants in the grass, running rapidly and purposefully about their business. Pausing to watch them I studied the form of their activity, wondering how much of their own pattern they were able to see for themselves. All at once I knew that I was so large that, to them, I was invisible — except, perhaps, as a shadow over their lives. I was gigantic, huge — able at one glance to comprehend, at least to some extent, the work of the whole colony. I had the power to destroy or scatter it, and I was completely outside the sphere of their knowledge and understanding. They were part of the body of the earth. But they knew nothing of the earth except the tiny part of it which was their home.

Turning away from them to my surroundings, I saw there was a tree not far away, and the sun was shining. There were clouds, and blue sky that went on for ever and ever. And suddenly I was tiny — so little and weak and insignificant that it didn't really matter at all whether I existed or not. And yet, insignificant as I was, my mind was capable of understanding that the limitless world I could see was beyond my comprehension. I could know myself to be a minute part of it all. I could understand my lack of understanding.

A watcher would have to be incredibly big to see me and the world around me as I could see the ants and their world, I thought. Would he think me to be as unaware of his existence as I knew the ants were of mine? He would have to be vaster than the world and space, and beyond understanding, and yet I *could* be aware of him — I *was* aware of him, in spite of my limitations. At the same time he was, and he was not, beyond my understanding.

Although my flash of comprehension was thrilling and transforming, I knew even then that in reality it was no more than a tiny glimmer. And yet, because there was this glimmer of understanding, the door of eternity was already open. My own part, however limited it might be, became in that moment a reality and must be included in the whole. In fact, the whole could not be complete without my own particular contribution. I was at the same time so insignificant as to be almost non-existent and so important that without me the whole could not reach fulfilment.

Every single person was a part of a Body, the purpose of which was as much beyond my comprehension now as I was beyond the comprehension of the ants. I was enchanted. Running indoors, delighted with my discovery, I announced happily, "We're like ants, running about on a giant's tummy!" No one understood, but that was unimportant. I knew what I knew.

It was a lovely thing to have happened. All my life, in times of great pain or distress or failure, I have been able to look back and remember, quite sure that the present agony was not the whole picture and that my understanding of it was limited as were the ants in their comprehension of their part in the world I knew.

This inner knowledge was exciting and absorbingly interesting, but it remained unsaid because, even if I could have expressed it, no one would have understood. Once, when I tried, I was told I was morbid. (F.55)

Descriptions like these raise all sorts of questions. How reliable, for a start, are such records? This one was written some 50 years after the incident described. How far can we really trust it as a historical record? I shall consider this problem later, and show also how I invited our correspondents to consider it. But there is something else.

"All my life I have been able to look back and remember . . ." The very reason for our misgivings, the deep and continuing involvement of the writer in the events she is recording, suggests another quite different line of thought. It is one thing to question this as an objective and detached record of a particular event and the feelings attached to it at the time. But by concentrating our critical attention on this problem (to which I see no solution) we may be missing something more important. What has been the nature of this process that was set going by that early event, or of the faculty that has enabled it to continue? To answer "childhood" to each of these questions is perhaps merely to overload a simple concept by confusing particular circumstances with longer-term consequences. But, unless we think purely in chronological terms, childhood can never be a simple concept. In existentialist terms it is a mystery not a problem, and mere dissection will do nothing to illuminate it. As I say, these complexities only began to come home to me in the course of the inquiry.

My immediate concern was to follow up all those, about 500, who had mentioned some childhood experience, and put to them a number of questions. I hoped they would say more about these experiences and the ideas and feelings associated with them. Also I wanted them to face the doubts that any intelligent sceptic would have about the reliability of their memories and their interpretations of them. The response to this questionnaire (which is given at the beginning of the appendix) was so rich and varied that for some time all that seemed necessary was to let our correspondents speak for themselves. The picture of childhood that emerged was lively and consistent; it would surely carry conviction by itself. I have in fact given a good deal of space at the end of Chapters 2 to 10 to quotations both from the original correspondence and from the answers to the follow-up inquiry. In an earlier draft of this book even greater prominence was given to this material. Friendly critics objected. Too much of it, they said, was commonplace. Reluctantly I conceded: they had a point. But so did I.

I have not yet paid my respects to William James, a thing that every writer on this subject must do, and sooner rather than later. *The Varieties of Religious Experience* is remarkable not merely for the lucidity, imaginative sympathy and brilliance of description with which he handles so extraordinary a range of human feeling and experience (as well as the candour with which he reveals his own blind spots[10]) but for the sheer vitality and freshness of his writing: the "Conclusions" and "Postscript" still make many present-day publications seem flabby in comparison, and I myself have often picked him up and been compelled to read on, and on, wondering how I could possibly have anything more to say. Still it must be pointed out that something at least of his magnetic readability is owed to his choice of examples. "I sought my documents", he says, "among the extravagances of the subject."[11] He believed, that is, that religious experience could best be illuminated by the study of its extreme forms. And so he deliberately selected cases that were "most one-sided, exaggerated and intense".[12] However, he was too honest an observer not to appreciate that what ultimately carries authority in religious experience is generally not its more sensational or dramatic manifestations but rather the quiet, unspectacular persistence of feelings that cannot for ever be denied. *Gutta cavat lapidem non vi sed saepe cadendo:* what counts in the end is neither the thunder nor the fire but the still small voice. Striking examples of "peak experiences" can easily be found, but the important thing is that they are only peaks, extreme instances of a capacity for spiritual understanding that is more commonly represented by slow and unobtrusive growth than by sudden confrontation or overwhelming conversion. Part, then, of my purpose is to suggest that religious experience is really something quite ordinary, commonplace if you like. So if you find nothing so very extraordinary in my examples, I will not say that was my intention, but it was a risk that had to be taken to make my point.

In this book, therefore, I am really trying to do two things. I want to do justice to the various aspects of childhood experience that are described in these accounts. But arising from them are other more fundamental issues to which I shall from time to time recur. Points on a graph must be plotted with reference to scales, vertical and horizontal, which give it meaning. So in the study of childhood experience there are, for me, certain concepts and categories which have this regulative function. But, as any researcher knows, evidence can be found for almost any thesis by selecting cases that support it and ignoring things that do not. So it is important here to show that the conclusions I reach are based not only on particular examples but on the general tendency of the material as a whole. It is for this purpose and no other that numerical analyses of the answers to each question are given in the appendix. Whether these 360 or so correspondents (or indeed the much larger number from which they were chosen) are representative of the country as a whole is another matter. Further research now in progress in the Nottingham

University School of Education will before long enable us to give some answer to that question.

In the following chapters, then, I shall be looking at the particular topics I asked our correspondents to reflect on. But all the time I shall have at the back of my mind some more general questions. These will come to the surface for explicit discussion at the appropriate times. I will briefly summarise them here.

I believe that what I have called "the original vision" of childhood is no mere imaginative fantasy but a form of *knowledge* and one that is essential to the development of any mature understanding.

I believe that this vision is related to what is often imprecisely described as *mystical* experience, though the latter phrase may include a great deal more than what is commonly experienced in childhood and is anyway too vague and emotive to be useful in this context.

I believe that this vision is one that can only properly be understood when studied *over a period of time*: that it is in fact to be included in the Aristotelian category of "natural" things which "move continuously by virtue of a principle inherent in themselves towards a determined goal".[13]

I believe that many of these childhood experiences are *self-authenticating:* they have in themselves an absolute authority that needs no confirmation or sanction from any other source.

I believe that they are also self-authenticating in another sense: they bring to the person who has them an awareness of his true *self* as an individual, with an identity, freedom and responsibilities of his or her own.

I believe that this vision can only be understood, either by the person who has it or by the outside observer, in *purposive* terms: there seems here no substitute for the old-fashioned word "destiny" — which however must be clearly distinguished from "fate".

And I believe finally that this vision and the experiences which are associated with it are essentially *religious,* and that no understanding, let alone definition, of that word is possible without a sympathetic insight into all that is here included in the concept of childhood.

A cultivated gentleman of the eighteenth century would sometimes take with him into the country a piece of equipment known as a "Claude glass". When looked at through this the English countryside would be seen in the remote and golden perspective of a classical Italian landscape; its homely features would take on the mellow grandeur of a painting by Claude Lorrain. This artificial substitute for a creative imagination produced nothing but a sentimental idealization of reality. The same thing can happen when the years of childhood are viewed in the perspective of age. But one can move too far in the other direction. To take childhood apart and analyse its components one by one may be no less inappropriate. I may at times seem to be doing this: to be offering a sort of "identikit" picture of a subject that is only recognizable as a unity. I can only hope that the result will help a sympathetic imagination to recreate for itself a more realistic image of that original vision.

2

VISION AND REALITY

Vision: the word will not appeal to the tough-minded: those who like to think of themselves as down-to-earth realists. It has ancient associations with dreams; it may suggest hallucinations, or some form of psychic awareness, what in some parts is still called "the sight". The visionary may be respected, even revered, as one of greater than normal powers, a "seer": where there is no vision, we are told, the people perish. Or he may be derided as an impractical dreamer, a victim of fantasy living in a world of his own. It may seem unfortunate to use the word to denote the particular gift of childhood. Children can live happily, it seems, in a world of make-believe: a tree stump without the slightest difficulty becomes a rocket launching-pad, and outer space as familiar as the way home from school. The sheer volatility of imagination with which they conceive the impossible is beyond most adults, until the time comes when they, the children that is, are taught to think sensibly and keep to the point, their minds disciplined along lines that will enable them to get on in our "real" world. What then is this "original vision" of childhood? Is there any reality that it corresponds to? Is it of any importance?

Look again at that account quoted on pp. 12f. Consider particularly the writer's claim to "understanding". She was very sure of herself. She still is. Her experience came as "a flash of comprehension". This last word is significant: it means taking everything together, making sense of the whole. At times there seems something almost mystical about this childhood comprehension, like the *"tota simul omnium possessio"* of Boethius, the complete possession of everything at one and the same time; or, as Edwin Muir put it, "a completer harmony of all things with each other than he will ever know again".[1] What has this to do with the reasoned understanding of mature thought, which not only knows but can say why it knows? More than we may at first suspect. The work of the discursive intellect, distinguishing one concept from another, and by an analytical process seeing relationships between the parts that form the whole — this was described by Plato in the *Phaedrus* as the double activity of dialectic: *dihaeresis* and *sunagoge,* taking things apart and bringing them together.[2] And this capacity for *sunagoge,* for synthesis, is, I will not say none other than, but certainly closely related to the capacity of the child for imaginative comprehension so clearly illustrated in this account, and many others like it.

If we are still inclined to see something fanciful in this association of the unitive vision of childhood with the processes of inductive reasoning, consider what Henri Poincaré wrote on the creative process in mathematical thought.[3] He speaks of "a special aesthetic sensibility" as indispensable for real creative achievement, and of the need for "the feeling of mathematical beauty, of the harmony of numbers and forms". What then are these mathematical entities which evoke in us this emotion?

> They are those whose elements are harmoniously disposed so that the mind without effort can embrace their totality while realizing the details. This harmony is at once a satisfaction of our aesthetic needs and an aid to the mind, sustaining and guiding. And at the same time, in putting under our eyes a well-ordered whole, it makes us foresee a mathematical law. Now, as we have said above, the only mathematical facts worthy of fixing our attention and capable of being useful are those which can teach us a mathematical law. So that we reach the following conclusion: The useful combinations are precisely the most beautiful, I mean those best able to charm this special sensibility that all mathematicians know, but of which the profane are so ignorant as often to be tempted to smile at it.

This is not to deny that the capacity for analytical and combinative thought will not generally appear until the years of childhood are over. The developmental psychologists are on firm ground here. What is more questionable is how this *synthetic* comprehension, in which the parts are seen in a logical relationship to the whole, relates to the *holistic* comprehension of childhood, in which that logical constructivism plays no part. Unfortunately the terms "cognitive" and "cognition" are now often kept for the synthetic process by psychologists who recognize no other. Thus Elkind, a follower of Piaget, writes of the "cognitive need capacities" that emerge at different stages of mental development, and of religion as offering "ready-made solutions" to the intellectual problems that arise at successive ages. From this "cognitive" point of view it may be that "the discovery that objects are conserved" is the most important accomplishment of the first two years of human life. But does it necessarily follow that God is then accepted as "the ultimate conservation since he transcends the bounds of space, time and corporality"? That such a sequence of ideas may sometimes occur is not in question; but not everyone, I imagine, will be satisfied with this sort of explanation of "the origins of religion in the child".[4]

"I knew what I knew". Knowing is not just thinking, having a fair idea, feeling pretty sure, or anything else short of certainty. Knowing is having no doubts at all. What is more, if you know, you are right. Of course she may have only thought she knew: she may have been wrong, but the idea never entered her head, either at the time or subsequently. So not only were these experiences real; they were experiences, we are constantly assured, of something real. You may say of course that this reality is primarily in the mind of the person having the experience; it is subjective. But this gives us no right to dismiss the experience; all our experience has subjective as well as objective elements in it. One or other may at times predominate; to call an experience "wholly subjective" is never justifiable. So let us leave this emotive pair of words and briefly consider what we mean by "real".

We used to hear a good deal of "coherence" and "correspondence" theories of truth. Something was true if it was in harmony with, or did not conflict with, other established "truths". How did they get to be established? By the same test of "coherence". This obviously was not enough. So for an idea to be true it also had to "correspond" with reality: there had to be something "out there" for it to match up with. How far do the experiences of childhood so often recounted to us pass these two tests? We have no way of telling, other than by noting what people say. And two things they do say are these. First, that again and again these experiences stood the test of time. The "reality" at which they hinted did prove to be really there; its existence was confirmed by subsequent experience. And the second is that they made sense in themselves; not only did they not conflict with other experiences, the picture they gave of the world was coherent; it was comprehensive in the sense discussed above. But in addition to "coherence" and "correspondence" what most directly carries conviction in so many of these experiences is something less amenable to analysis. It is what I can only call immediacy. "It was as if something said to me, 'Don't ever allow yourself to question this.' And I knew that I mustn't; I knew it was the most real thing that had ever happened to me." Now this is a very curious thing to say. What can it mean to call some things more real than others? Let us take another look at this word.

Most commonly we use it in a no-nonsense way to distinguish between the genuine and the false. "Come off it: either it's real silk or it isn't". The alternatives are plain; it must be one or the other. But we sometimes speak as though there were degrees of reality, particularly in things whose true nature or potential is in some way mysterious to us. In this sense a dream may be unusually "real": a character in a book may have this same quality. And this is not just because either the dream or the character is exceptionally life-like, though this may be one reason for its power over us. Tolstoy's Anna is not just a wonderfully realistic figure; her "reality" lies in her power to reveal to us, if we can take it, something about the whole nature of woman. The fact is that certain circumstances, certain experiences make a particular *demand* upon us; we are called on to respond at a depth we hardly knew existed in us. The great composers, the great writers, the great artists have this gift; their

21

works confront us, though not of course inescapably, because we can always pass on to something more comfortable, something less charged with reality. "A painting for me," says Ben Nicholson, "if it's anything is a living thing and should achieve a form of life more real than life itself."

Then we use the word in a purely pragmatic sense: "That's what I call a real fire;" it does what a fire should do. So of our own experiences. There are unquestionably moments in the lives of each of us that come home to us with a special, quite penetrating significance ("Don't ever allow yourself to question this . . .") because they seem to have an essentially *functional* importance; they are not only startlingly "real" in themselves but they are a momentary revelation to us of what it really means to be alive. And not only that; they are like batteries which, when kept topped up and occasionally recharged, are a source of power and light for the future. Maslow may have been a little indiscriminate in including so great a range within his "peak experiences", but to me at least he is totally convincing in his insistence that it is at these moments that the human individual is most really operative. Psychology has far too long been obsessed with the "reality" of pathological states and processes: if you want to know what a real man is like, he says, find one that is working properly. There is nothing really new in this; it goes back to the "entelechy" of Aristotle. He may not have been the first existentialist, but at least he appreciated that a purely static view of reality could do no justice to human experience.

So there are a great many ways in which we use the word "real" to describe the object of our experience, and it is often in the most profound and mysterious of these senses that it occurs in these accounts of childhood. This vision then comes in the form of knowledge, and its content appears unquestionably real, often intensely so: the experience may come, as one writer says, as "a diamond moment of reality". Another writes, "If it was hallucination, why do I remember it as the most real and living experience that I have ever had? It was like contacting a live wire when you were groping for a match." If what is communicated at times like these is to be dismissed as unreal, then what is to be believed? Can experiences so vivid and compelling be dismissed

22

as the product of fantasy, imagination or daydream?

Yes, of course they can. Plenty of experiences bring with them an intensely vivid impression of reality. Dreams and certain drug induced states can be compellingly "real". And a dream *is* real in its own way; it is a real dream, just as a hallucination is a real hallucination. It is only in taking one level of reality for another that delusion lies. The argument from immediacy is by itself quite unreliable; only when it is supported by evidence of coherence and correspondence is it convincing. Support of this kind is, as I hope to show, available. First though I must deal briefly with some other criticisms. There are in fact all sorts of ways in which without seeming too ungenerous or sceptical we can quietly undermine the claims that these otherwise disturbing records may make on us.

The question of the reliability of memory I have already mentioned. An even more basic one concerns the possibility of fraud. How do we know that all these impressive accounts are not just cooked up for our benefit? The question has come up regularly in discussion; even the tone of voice is predictable. The possibility that there is something here that must be taken seriously is clearly felt as some kind of threat; to question the authenticity of the records is the first and most obvious defence. When maintained with resolution there is no way past such scepticism. All I can say is that both in reading the original contributions (represented generally here by only short extracts) and in following them up either by further correspondence or by meeting their writers I have never had any doubts that proved justified. The conclusions I myself have drawn may sometimes be speculative, where our correspondents have left room between the lines: I may from time to time have misread their intentions, but never I am sure their basic seriousness of purpose.

Then again, it is possible to feel that these experiences may well have occurred much as they are described, but that to understand them properly you must know more about the upbringing, environment and so on of the people who record them. Fair enough: obviously there are psychological and cultural influences at work on each one of us all the time. And in childhood, it may be, we are especially open to them. The way we are brought up, the society we live in, not to mention heredity — all these things shape our experience and even more the way we describe it. It is no good denying all this, but it is none the less possible to accept it all and still feel that the experience even of children (and why "even"?) cannot be wholly explained without remainder in such terms. I discuss these questions, and the ways I asked our correspondents to consider them, in Chapters 5, 6 and 7.

First of all though I want to face another question. We may accept these accounts as basically authentic; we may feel that things happened much as they are described. We may accept the experiences recorded as having an element at least of spontaneity or autonomy, that is, as being not wholly derived from external factors. And yet after all we may not find them very impressive or significant. Why? The fact is that many of these childhood experiences seem to belong to a world that is for ever closed to most of us; and this makes us all the more ready to find some reason for discrediting them, or at least for not taking them seriously. For some it is enough to describe them as "visionary". Others will call them "mystical", a term which to some people is in itself sufficient to suggest that they have little to do with the real business of life. "The words 'mysticism' and 'mystical' ", wrote William James, "are often used as terms of mere reproach, to throw at any opinion which we regard as vague and vast and sentimental, and without a base in either facts or logic."[5] Precisely: it is very difficult to use these words without provoking resistance in somebody or other. Mysticism has been associated, however ignorantly, with the occult, the psychic, the subjective, the irrational, the woolly-minded, and now in our own time with psychedelic drugs and the altered states of consciousness business. In the church it has been suspect for various reasons. It has seemed to offer a private source for spiritual truth, and so to threaten orthodoxy, and to a good protestant, as Bishop Butler said to John Wesley, "the pretending to extraordinary revelations and gifts of the Holy Ghost is a horrid thing, a very horrid thing". And then mysticism has often supported a pantheistic view of reality, and this is seen

24

as undermining morality. (It was for this reason that a professor of education in one of our ancient universities described our whole programme of research as "trivial and irrelevant".) All this will show why I generally avoid the word "mystical" and its associated forms; it will also show why it comes so easily to many otherwise sensible English men and women to dismiss as "mystical" many of the more striking experiences of young children.

This is a pity, for in fact James had a pretty clear idea in his own mind of what would justify us in calling an experience "mystical". His criteria are lucid, and his descriptions brilliant. Of the "noetic" aspect of these experiences he wrote: "They are states of insight into depths of truth unplumbed by the discursive intellect. They are illuminations, revelations, full of significance and importance, all inarticulate though they remain; and as a rule they carry with them a curious sense of authority for after-time."[6] The precision of this description can be confirmed again and again in our material; it will surely be recognized in the examples I quote. All the same, I prefer to avoid so emotive and loaded a word. And there is another reason.

When Sir Alister Hardy first faced the massive task of sorting out this very heterogeneous correspondence, which covers just about any aspect of religious, spiritual, psychic, transcendental or paranormal experience that you care to name, he wondered at first whether it would help to set up two provisional categories: "A" for those whose experience took the form of a steady, more or less continuous sense of spiritual or religious awareness, and "B" for those who reported a more particularised, often sensational or ecstatic, "mystical" kind of experience: something suddenly breaking in from outside into the tenor of life, in contrast to the "A" type of experience which was more to be identified with life itself. The division, predictably enough it now seems, was not practicable. This is not to say that it would not be perfectly easy, without very much dishonesty, to put together an impressive body of cases suggesting that there *were* two distinct types of experience. I can think of several recent studies of particular kinds of what may broadly be described as religious phenomena, well researched and persuasively presented, which fail to carry conviction only with those who know that for every clear cut case of X or Y there are several others that almost qualify, or fall between the two, or are so bewilderingly diverse as to exemplify two mutually incompatible characteristics at one and the same time. So with our "A" and "B". To begin with, we had to realize that much probably remained unsaid. Then even in what we had it was not always possible to say with any confidence that this element or that was or was not represented. It is a good thing to be reminded by writers like Von Hügel and Otto and now in our own time by Ninian Smart what a rich and complex thing religion is; but the chief value of their analyses is that they remind us that none of these factors or elements or dimensions should be ignored either in judging a religion as a whole or in examining the experience of an individual.

I should add here that one need not actually describe as dishonest such books as Ben-Ami Scharfstein's *Mystical Experience* (though a man who ends up by admitting "I myself dislike and prefer to explain away much of mysticism"[7] can hardly be called a sympathetic or even a detached observer). But we fall too easily into the habit of speaking of "mystics" as though they were a distinct type of human being, almost a mutation, endowed with some special faculty, some particular sensitivity the rest of us lack. True, in most cultures those who have been more gifted than others in this respect have been singled out, and often trained, as seers or shamans; but it does not follow that such men are different in kind from their fellows. More often the allocation of this particular role is part of the general division of labour: the job of being a spiritual lightning-conductor is one that is gladly deputed to the man or woman best qualified, to the general benefit, and relief, of the rest of the community.

The peculiar vision of childhood, then, may be called mystical if you like, but not if this word is used to suggest that that vision is essentially irrational, romantic, impractical or unreal. On the contrary, the child's view of the world is often more realistic and a good less sentimental than that of many adults; this will come out strongly in Chapter 9, and I hope elsewhere. (Only if you equate realism with materialism does the adult have a clear advantage). There is however one apparently distinct form of experience for which no word other than "mystical" seems appropriate; and as it is commonly reported from childhood it requires more particular attention. This is what is commonly called "Nature Mysticism". This I leave to the next chapter.

*　　　*　　　*

Further Examples

Comprehension

I think from my childhood I have always had the feeling that the true reality is not to be found in the world, as the average person sees it. There seems to be a constant force at work from the inside trying to push its way to the surface of consciousness. The mind is continually trying to create a symbol sufficiently comprehensive to contain it, but this always ends in failure. There are moments of pure joy with a heightened awareness of one's surroundings, as if a great truth had been passed across . . . At times it feels that the physical brain is not big enough·to let it through.

(M. 42)

Until I was seven, religion was purely external, expressed perhaps by the nursery jingle "One, two, three, four, five, six, seven, All good children go to Heaven", reinforced by hymns of the infant school, such as "All things bright and beautiful", "There is a green hill", etc. Then in Standard II of a Wesleyan School I had an extraordinarily vivid insight which is absolutely beyond description but which has remained with me ever since as an abiding spiritual experience. The teacher was explaining that in addition to common nouns and proper nouns there were also abstract nouns, which mostly ended in "-ness", such as goodness, badness, etc: also a number of short but very important

27

words such as love, hate, etc. It was at this point that I seemed to grow up mentally. The fact that it was completely ineffable does not puzzle me in the least since it appears to have been a common experience of contemplatives to be unable to find words to describe what they have inwardly experienced. You ask how it may have affected one's life. All I can say is that it has served as an inescapable sense of assurance through a life of average mixture of pleasant and unpleasant experiences, doubts and fears.

(M. 75)

Immediacy

As a small child one of my favourite festivals was Trinity Sunday. It seemed to me quiet and beautiful, and happening about midsummer became associated in my mind with green trees and flowers in bloom. It was "mysterious" and right, something far bigger than the words used in church about it which sounded to a small child nonsense. But Trinity wasn't nonsense, it was Holy, holy, holy, as we sang in the hymn, and even a very young child could join in a sort of "oneness" with all things bright and beautiful and worship this Something so great and lovely that it didn't matter at all that it was also not understood. It just WAS. (F. 64)

The Sense of Meaning

I had my first religious experience when I was about six and saw the whole evening sky covered by small, criss-cross, clearly defined and vividly coloured rainbow pieces. At about ten years of age I saw the entire evening sky filled with meteorites which fell like snowflakes all about me. Both sights seemed to me at the time to represent objective natural events. Only much later did I realise that they must have been purely subjective experiences. Both caused me to feel overwhelmed by an awareness of the awesome beauty of nature, as if I had been granted a glimpse of a state of absolute beauty, absolute perfection, and a meaning behind daily events which was incomprehensible to my intellect but is nevertheless deeply ingrained in my memory.

(F. 46)

The Sense of Unity

There was yet another feeling that used to come over me which now I can only call a kind of insight. At the time, when I was a child, I only remember the feeling as one of intense reality and knowing, a sort of grown-up feeling when I really saw and knew how things really were underneath appearances. At these times of knowing I did not see quivering colours, nor feel huge, nor hear strange inner hums; but rather I saw the ordinary world very clearly and in infinite details, and knew it to be all joined up, and all made of one primal substance or life force, which force whipped up the poles of duality: this produced electricity and polarity, and thus was formed every atom and every material thing. I could see how we are all one substance and interdependent, and all joined, and how in reality nothing has a fixed immovable edge or skin, but all things merge into their surroundings.

I learned very young that appearances are deceptive, and that the finite conception of things as this and that is an idea peculiar and appropriate to man, who has named all the apparently separate things he has seen ever since he evolved sufficiently to introduce language and to see the power of the word. A child has no means of knowing if he feels differently from other people or not. As I grew up I was ever more perplexed to realise that many people lived in a world quite different from my own. They could kill things without hurting themselves, they could sleep without dreaming, or dream without colours. They could apparently always feel themselves to be inside their skins, and the things they saw and heard and felt seemed real and separate and distinct realities. The objective world seemed real to most people, and the subjective world unreal or nonexistent.

This kind of insight, though so difficult to describe, took place in the deepest part of me and seemed to be the least dependent upon the senses. I understood without seeing, and what I saw or heard or touched seemed to be of secondary importance to what I knew. When I was a child I would experience it suddenly, and then suddenly lose it again, perhaps after only a few seconds or minutes. The awareness of unity only came over me infrequently when I was a child as far as I can remember. As I grew up it became more frequent, and nowadays it has become almost continuous when I am alone or in contemplative mood. I like this feeling, and often leave the ordinary awareness of duality and harsh definition to enter at will into the rolling awareness of the unity and edgelessness of reality.

(F. 49)

3

"NATURE MYSTICISM"

It may in general be said that the particular trigger of an experience, the immediate cause or circumstances that set it off, may have no significant relation to the experience itself. This rule applies to all kinds of experience. You can if you like collect cases of experience that have occurred in the course of, or as a result of, going to church. What will they have in common? Probably very little. Cultural influences will be strong; that is to say, the language used, the categories of thought, will be generally determined by the religious beliefs or upbringing of the writers. Often it is impossible to see through the fog of religious cliché — sin, salvation, redemption and so forth — to form any clear or distinctive idea of what the person really felt. Even so, it soon becomes apparent that to attempt to correlate the considerable variety of experience recorded with the particular circumstances in which it occurred is a largely artificial exercise. The thing is hardly worth doing. It would be no less significant, and probably much more entertaining, to appeal to people for accounts of ideas, feelings or inspirations that had come to them in the bath. The same rule applies, I suspect, to such artificially induced experiences as LSD trips or other deliberately altered states of consciousness. I speak with caution here as I have not made a specialized study, but there are such close parallels between examples of these and others of quite spontaneous experiences that I shall take a lot of convincing that the actual trigger has any diagnostic value.

So it is with "nature". Wordsworth's profound eloquence in telling of that

> sense sublime
> Of something far more deeply interfused,
> Whose dwelling is the light of setting suns,
> And the round ocean and the living air,
> And the blue sky, and in the mind of man,[1]

may for a moment convince us that this deeply felt pantheistic experience can be put into a class by itself, a mysticism peculiarly of nature. But Wordsworth himself gives the answer to this, with his quaint account of a timeless moment on the top of a London bus:

> On the roof
> Of an itinerant vehicle I sate,
> With vulgar men about me, trivial forms
> Of houses, pavements, streets, of men and things —
> Mean shapes on every side.

Yet still it came — "with Time it dwells, and grateful memory, as a thing divine".[2] His poetry, however, is so splendid that we may not realise how remarkably imprecise he is in actually describing what happened to him. I sometimes read of "the Wordsworthian experience", but really the phrase will not do — unless that is, like R. C. Zaehner, you write only to discredit it.[3]

This in fact is the last thing I want to do. Especially for small children, the first impact of the beauty of nature can be quite overwhelming. To be patronizing or cynical about these experiences may be one defence against having to take them seriously. What we must surely not do is question that "curious sense of authority for after-time" that remains with those that have them. Yet the actual content of the experience, if one can make that distinction, the actual truth that comes home, the seed that is planted, later perhaps to germinate but always to be true in specific characters to that original moment — all this may vary tremendously. Consider three specific cases.

Through the spring, summer and autumn days from about the age of seven, I would sit alone in my little house in the tree tops observing all nature around me and the sky overhead at night. I was too young to be able to think and reason in the true sense but with the open receptive mind of a young, healthy boy I slowly became aware of vague, mysterious laws in everything around me. I must have become attuned to nature. I felt these laws of life and movement so deeply they seemed to saturate my whole mind and body, yet they always remained just beyond my grasp and understanding.

(M. 68)

The most profound experience of my life came to me when I was very young — between four and five years old. I am not mistaken in dating this because I remember so clearly both the place where it occurred and the shoes I was wearing at the time, of which I was rather fond. Both of these facts relate only to this particular period in my life; I have a dated photograph of myself wearing the shoes in question.

My mother and I were walking on a stretch of land in Pangbourne Berks, known locally as "the moors". As the sun declined and the slight chill of evening came on, a pearly mist formed over the ground. My feet, with the favourite black shoes with silver buckles, were gradually hidden from sight until I stood ankle deep in gently swirling vapour. Here and there just the very tallest harebells appeared above the mist. I had a great love of these exquisitely formed flowers, and stood lost in wonder at the sight.

Suddenly I seemed to see the mist as a shimmering gossamer tissue and the harebells, appearing here and there, seemed to shine with a brilliant fire. Somehow I understood that this was the living tissue of life itself, in which that which we call consciousness was embedded, appearing here and there as a shining focus of energy in the more diffused whole. In that moment I knew that I had my own special place, as had all other things, animate and so-called inanimate, and that we were all part of this universal tissue which was both fragile yet immensely strong, and utterly good and beneficent.

The vision has never left me. It is as clear today as fifty years ago, and with it the same intense feeling of love of the world and the certainty of ultimate good. It gave me then a strong, clear sense of identify which has withstood many vicissitudes, and an affinity with plants, birds, animals, even insects, and people too, which has often been commented upon. Moreover, the whole of this experience has ever since formed a kind of reservoir of strength fed from an unseen source, from which quite suddenly in the midst of the very darkest times a bubble of pure joy rises through it all, and I know that whatever the anguish there is some deep centre in my life which cannot be touched by it.

Of course, at the early age of four or five I could not have expressed anything of the experience in the words I have now used, and perhaps the attempt to convey the absorption of myself into the whole, and the intensity of meaning, sounds merely over-coloured to the reader. But the point is that, by whatever mysterious perception, the whole impression and its total meaning were apprehended in a single instant. Years later, reading Traherne and Meister Eckhart and Francis of Assisi, I have cried aloud with surprise and joy, knowing myself to be in the company of others who had shared the same kind of experience and who had been able to set it down so marvellously. This is not the only experience of the kind that has come to me — indeed they occur relatively often — but it is without doubt the one which has laid the deepest foundations of my life, and for which I feel the profoundest gratitude.

(F. 57)

The first approach to a spiritual experience which I can remember must have taken place when I was five or six years old at the house where I was born and brought up. It was a calm, limpid summer morning and the early mist still lay in wispy wreaths among the valleys. The dew on the grass seemed to sparkle like iridescent jewels in the sunlight, and the shadows of the houses and trees seemed friendly and protective. In the heart of the child that I was there suddenly seemed to well up a deep and overwhelming sense of gratitude, a sense of unending peace and security which seemed to be part of the beauty of the morning, the love and protective and living presence which included all that I had ever loved and yet was something much more.

(M. 63)

Here are three people, each of whom as a small child many years ago underwent an experience in the face of "nature" that left him or her with a profound sense of mystery. For each, as for Wordsworth, what he or she experienced eluded precise

33

description. What else do they have in common? Not a great deal. To the first the mystery presents itself principally as an intellectual problem. It was "just beyond my grasp". He was conscious of "vague mysterious laws" that challenged his understanding. In a subsequent passage he goes on to tell how he "grew up with one overwhelming aim in life, to solve the meaning of these mysterious laws". (He later became a writer, first on Marxism and later on Theosophy). The second describes the mystery in what might be called organic or structural terms: "I understood that this was the living tissue of life itself in which that which we call consciousness was embedded." There is also a powerful sense of aesthetic precision, reflected in her case not only in a telling lucidity of phrase but also in a very fine, and finely controlled, handwriting. (She later trained as an art teacher, and became an authority on the development of architecture.) In the third account the language of personal feeling and relationships is dominant; the writer speaks of "an overwhelming sense of gratitude", of "love" and "friendliness", of "a protective and living presence". (He grew up to be a management consultant and an adviser on industrial relations.) Can one say that these three experiences fall into the same category? If one knew more about the writers than I do, or am in a position to tell, it would I think become clear that the actual experience, what it meant for each, the impulse that the life of each one received from it, was subtly different. What was significant about the experience was the way in which it helped each to become the person he or she had it in him or her to become. That the beauty of nature started it all off is incidental.

I said something in the previous chapter about "mysticism", and the dangers of letting ourselves be put off by a label that might suggest something esoteric or remote from daily life. I should like to end this one by taking a rather closer look at an episode that on its own might be thought fairly trivial: an example perhaps of how a small incident in unusual circumstances can appeal to the sense of wonder of a sensitive and impressionable child.

As a child (not younger than 6, not older than 8), I had an experience which nowadays I consider as kindred, if not identical, with those experiences related by Wordsworth in The Prelude, Bk. 1, lines 379-400. The circumstances were: dusk, summertime, and I one of a crowd of grown-ups and children assembled round the shore of a large ornamental lake, waiting for full darkness before a firework display was to begin. A breeze stirred the leaves of a group of poplars just to my right; stirred, they gave a fluttering sound. There, then, I knew or felt or experienced — what? Incommunicable now, but then much more so. The sensations were of awe or wonder, and a sense of astounding beauty — at that moment in dusk — and the perception that *it* would have gone when it was dark and the fireworks began. And so it was. I remember exactly the place where the experience occurred and have since often revisited it, at various hours, but nothing of quite the same kind (despite a host of intense experiences of different kinds since) happened again. That child of 6 or 7 or 8 knew nothing of Wordsworth or about mysticism or about religion.

(M. 55)

A few years ago while working for a television programme I met the writer of this account. We talked about his experience, and what it had continued to mean to him in later life. I quote from a tape of our conversation. He said:

It's very difficult to say that it revealed — what? The existence of infinity? The fact of divinity? I wouldn't have had the language at my command as a child to formulate such things, so that if I speak about it now it is with the language and ideas of a mature person. But from my present age, looking back some half a century, I would say now that I did then experience — what? a truth, a fact, the existence of the divine. What happened was telling me something. But what was it telling? The fact of divinity, that it was good? Not so much the moral sense, but that it was beautiful, yes, sacred.

We went on to talk about Wordworth and his sense of loss in later life. He quoted the passage from the well-known Ode:

We will grieve not;
Though nothing can bring back the hour
Of splendour in the grass,
Of glory in the flower,
We will grieve not, rather find
Strength in what remains behind,

> In the primal sympathy
> Which having been must ever be.

That expresses the kind of consolation that one has. And then there are the lines,

> But there's a tree, of many, one,
> A single field that I have looked upon,
> Both of them speak of something that is gone.

> It had gone, but it had been once, and he feels it must therefore ever be. Now when I read Wordsworth, when I read those lines, I am consoled.

It had gone; nevertheless it had left behind an assurance, a certainty. And that assurance was definitely of a religious kind, "a guarantee of the truth of the numinous". Though the feeling that originally went with it could not now be recreated, the memory of the event remained as a resource to be drawn on.

> One might say that recollection of it acts as a kind of tap-root to springs of life. It became very active, this early experience, very active in my mind some five years ago when I suffered a very great bereavement, the greatest I suppose that a man can have. And then this original experience was called upon by some part of my personality; it asserted itself and became very active. There was a strength there, a strength or comfort. It was an assurance, a guarantee. That I know.

It is hard enough to know what to think about the description of the single event from which all this grew; he admits that at the time he did not have the language to put his feelings into words. It is even more difficult to analyse what followed from it in terms of the mystical or the numinous or to describe it in religious or psychological categories. But more than that; it would be impertinent, because here we are looking at something that has become part of a man's life, has coloured and enriched all aspects of it. We may find it convenient for comparative purposes to call this an example of "nature mysticism", but we must not deceive ourselves into thinking that we have thereby said anything significant either about the experience itself or, still less, about what it meant to the human being who had it.

*   *   *

Further Examples

When I was about eleven years old I spent part of a summer holiday in the Wye Valley. Waking up very early one bright morning, before any of the household was about, I left my bed and went to kneel on the window-seat, to look out over the curve which the river took just below the house. The trees between the house and the river — I was on a level with their topmost branches — were either poplars or silver birch, and green fields stretched away beyond the river to the far distance. The morning sunlight shimmered on the leaves of the trees and on the rippling surface of the river. The scene was very beautiful, and quite suddenly I felt myself on the verge of a great revelation. It was as if I had stumbled unwittingly on a place where I was not expected, and was about to be initiated into some wonderful mystery, something of indescribable significance. Then, just as suddenly, the feeling faded. But for the brief seconds while it lasted I had known that in some strange way I, the essential "me", was a part of the trees, of the sunshine, and the river, that we all belonged to some great unity. I was left filled with exhilaration and exultation of spirit. This is one of the most memorable experiences of my life, of a quite different quality and greater intensity than the sudden lift of the spirit one may often feel when confronted with beauty in Nature.

(F. 40)

I did not attribute any great significance to these experiences: they were an expression of my ecstatic love of what Wordsworth calls "natural objects", not utterly different from the ecstasy of sexual love. I did not think of them in terms of union with God, for instance, until much later. I used to be puzzled by the way this experience would come unheralded, and in the most unlikely places — not, for instance, in rose plot, fringed pool, fern'd grot — but in a bus or by a dustbin; but I did not think a lot about it or try to give a meaning to it until I read Wordsworth, and, later still, various books on mysticism.

(F. 53)

4

THE CHILD THAT I USED TO BE

At the heart of all fidelity, says Gabriel Marcel, lies the ability to be faithful to oneself. "To thine own self be true": this has often been said, but does it mean more than the preservation of an inner integrity, the refusal to abandon convictions one has made one's own? Yes, says Marcel, because to be faithful to myself means to remain alive, which is not nearly as easy as it sounds. It means above all "not to be hypnotized by what I have achieved but on the contrary to get clear of it", that is, to go on living and find renewal.

> If I admit that to be faithful to myself means to be faithful to certain principles which I have adopted once and for all, I am in danger of introducing into my life as foreign, and we can even say as destructive, an element as the artist who copies himself does. It may quite well happen that these principles or these opinions end by covering up and stifling my own special reality; in that case, how am I to be faithful to myself? I am no longer there, I do not exist any more.

But what is this self to which I must be faithful? First of all it is something that must be kept alive; it must constantly be renewed. And secondly, that life, that renewal, has something to do with childhood.

> I tend to become increasingly profane in relation to a certain mystery of my *self* to which access is more and more strictly forbidden me. I should add that this unquestionably comes about in so far as the child that I used to be, and that I should have remained were I a poet, dies a little more each day.[1]

38

All this I can see will provoke some impatience in those who are still not convinced that the vision of childhood is anything more than a poetic fancy. For a great many of us, anyway, who have in years at least left childhood behind, if we ever had such a vision, it was for all practical purposes a "baseless fabric" which has left "not a wrack behind". And some people will tell us that this is as it should be. Few things certainly are more pathetic than the sentimental nostalgia that will not let go of the past, that wishes continually to return to an ideal world that probably never existed outside an imagination that takes refuge in it. What else, after all, is this world of fantasy but a means of escape from adult reality?

Freud was deeply interested in childhood. Regression to childhood could be a key to unlock the neurosis of maturity. Early memories repressed by the conscious mind could by patient excavation be brought to the surface. Events and experiences rooted deep in the oblivion of childhood could, he discovered, through dream and fantasy be brought to light. "Certain dreams convince me", says Muir, "that a child has this vision." Freud would have agreed. He would also have gone further; the vision, itself, he would have said, was the product of infantile frustration or imbalance. There is something inherently frustrating about human infancy, and the child's inevitable dissatisfaction with what Freud, like Piaget, would call without qualification the "real" world leads, so the argument goes, to a search for compensation. This results in the development of an inner world of fantasy, which may extend far beyond childhood. There can be few of us who have not at some time, when the complexities and responsibilities of life seem just too much for us, thought wistfully of those old simplicities.

That such flights of the imagination might lead in later life to the creation of great works of art, to the building of elaborate systems of philosophy or the exploration of profound spiritual experience, this was to Freud neither here nor there. He was honest enough to admit their value, at least in the case of literature: "The Brothers Karamazov," he wrote, "is the most magnificent novel ever written: the episode of the Grand Inquisitor, one of the peaks in the literature of the world, can hardly be valued too highly. Before the problem of the creative artist analysis must, alas, lay down its arms."[2] But speaking generally it was enough for Freud to have discovered, as he thought, what was the common origin of all these works of the creative imagination, to show what they all sprang from; and this, to him, was nothing more than infantile frustration. This done, to ask whether there was any transcendental reality they might represent, or even point to, was a question that was simply not worth asking. There was nothing more that needed to be explained. Reality lay not in these flights of fantasy but in the hard, gritty, unforgiving world we must eventually come to terms with. There is an old Bemba proverb: "The arrow in the air is only hunting: when it falls to earth it has come home". So much for this "original vision of the world", that "completer harmony of all things with each other" than we shall ever know again. It is born of frustration, nourished by nostalgia and due to end, if we do not watch it, in neurosis. The earth, not the sky, is our home.

There is a great deal to be learnt from Freud, just as there is a great deal to be learnt from Piaget. But it is important to recognize that all that they have discovered is strictly related to the questions from which they started. Erik Erikson puts the matter clearly. Writing as a psychologist, he acknowledges the need to learn from other branches of science, since "only through the inventive methodologies of these disciplines do we have knowledge at all. Unfortunately, however", he continues, "this knowledge is tied to the conditions under which it was secured."[3] In the cases he is there concerned with, "a scientific discipline prejudiced the matter under observation by actively dissolving its total living situation in order to make an isolated section of it amenable to a set of instruments or concepts." So we should not be overimpressed by either Piaget or Freud if we feel, as I do, that their insights are limited by their presuppositions. Piaget's concern was to establish how children develop into the intellectual maturity of adulthood. For this purpose his questions were the right ones: we now know a great deal more about this development. Freud was a doctor; he wanted to discover the causes of, and the cure for, certain forms of mental illness. Again, the questions he asked were, for him, the right ones: we know that much mental disturbance can be the result of the traumas of infancy and childhood, and can be treated by psychoanalytic methods that help the patient to come to terms with those early experiences. We owe a great deal to the "inventive methodologies" of these scientists. But it is no less scientific to insist on returning again and again to the "total living situation". So let us not be put off by these great reputations, and consider more deeply why Marcel should have regretted the death of the child within himself.

The charge of nostalgia is an easy one to bring against anyone who finds significance in childhood experience. How far is it deserved by those who have written to us? What made so many of them start by going back so far? Was it more than a romantic fantasy, a sentimental longing for an idealized simplicity, a lost innocence? If such were the real feelings of those we were relying on for our understanding of childhood, however conceived, the sooner we knew it the better. How did they now feel they related to those early experiences?

Not at all, for the most part, in this nostalgic spirit. At the heart of nostalgia lies an ache to return to the past, a past that is dead and gone. "O death in life", wrote Tennyson, "the days that are no more". To most of our correspondents, however, that past was still alive only in the sense that what had started then had gone on growing. Of all those approached (See Appendix, questions 8 and 9) nearly three quarters saw their childhood experiences as no more than the first steps in a process of growing awareness which was not to be complete until later, if then. Others found it hard to distinguish, in terms of vividness and significance, between early and subsequent experience: the continuity was more important to them than any sense of progression. Only a small minority (13%, and among the under 35s only 4%) felt that childhood had given them something more revealing than anything in later life. The pattern was much the same with both men and women. There is no general tendency here to idealize the years of childhood.

There is of course one advantage that childhood has over any later age: it sees things for the first time. The second time round

41

there can never be quite the same thrill in the simple pleasures of nature. There are those of course who take some time to lose this capacity. Wordsworth is the obvious example. Still, for all his ecstasies over the celandine and the daffodils, it was the sense of loss that he became most conscious of at last. It is not that we can no longer be moved by natural beauty. On the contrary, we may each year become more vulnerable to sights, sounds and smells that are loaded with associations, conscious or unconscious. But this is something different; it is "emotion recollected in tranquillity", not at all the same as the simple rapture of childhood. "I seemed then", says one, "to have a more direct relationship with flowers, trees and animals", and another, "I can remember vividly at eight or nine the sense of having lost 'participation mystique' with sunsets, the smell of wet grass, the life of trees and animals; there had passed away a glory from the earth." Then there are those few who, like Wordsworth again or Traherne, hint at an awareness of pre-natal memories, so that the beauties of this world seem at first sight no more than reminders of another. These two categories apart, though, it is rare to find any among these records that give a clear superiority either in vividness or in long-term significance to pre-adolescent experience.

Then there were those, as I have said, but again a minority, who record no real sense of growth, little more in fact than a sense of continuity. "I thought and felt as a child much as I think and feel now. Somehow my soul or inner self knows no age." Others in this group reject the idea that the kind of analysis I suggest can ever throw light on a whole which never grew bit by bit but always as an organic unity. To draw a circle you have to start at one particular point, but that is not the way to *conceive* a circle: its essential circularity exists independently of the way we construct the figure. If reality to a child is timeless, then the only understanding we can have of our childhood must come by our laying aside these time-bound constructs of relationship and measurement. This approach will hardly satisfy the developmental psychologist; and understandably enough, since one of his chief concerns is with the way we gradually acquire those powers of thought and analysis that tempt us to articulate a

42

reality whose essence passes like water through the finest of such nets. Articulate: a revealing word: "To connect by joints" (OED). A piece of string is inarticulate; it can wind itself round any shape you like, while we with our most finely articulated thought labour to piece together ever more intricate constructs to describe that most slippery and unpredictable of creatures, noble in reason but also infinite in faculty, that is man: meccano models of a whole universe of thought and feeling, some of them about as subtle or flexible as an articulated lorry. No wonder then that there are those who reject analysis from the start: "I feel an unchanging core of feeling, lasting to the end of time, because it is timeless. I sleep, I wake, ad infinitum."

This is a point of view that must be respected. Indeed it is more than just a point of view, it is an aspect of reality. All the same, it is one that only a minority emphasize. After all, we cannot entirely deny change as we leave the years of childhood behind. It is all very well to talk, as one correspondent does, of "the ebb and flow of an ever-present sea", but it is only through change that we become aware of continuity and vice versa. Most of them, therefore, while giving full credit to the sharpness and lucidity of the early vision — "a clear awareness, almost like radar" — have to admit that something has changed, and not always by any means for the worse. To use analytic language the vision of childhood has been preserved alongside the development of those other faculties we know so much more about. This is one way of looking at it. Brain surgery has made us familiar with the idea of localized functions, and this tempts us to think of the mind in the same way. The earlier depth psychologists would talk confidently about "the unconscious", even "the contents of the unconscious", and this sectional thinking, which goes back to Plato and no doubt beyond, has now acquired an almost scientific respectability. In fact it is difficult to avoid this kind of language; I find myself talking of childhood as a "faculty", which is really a very misleading word unless kept strictly in quotes. Adverbs are a clumsy substitute, but if we stick to "thinking unconsciously", "religiously", "analytically" and so forth we shall avoid some of the compartmental presuppositions in which our psychology so often gets entangled. For childhood though words fail us; there is no single adverb to describe the holistic simplicity that is so often characteristic of a child's thought. So we fall back on metaphor.

"Just as circles in a tree trunk make up the story of the tree's growth, so all that has happened in the religious development of an individual is never really discarded, but is incorporated in the whole pattern of living." This sort of language is frequent. Faced with this mysterious presence of a childhood still active at some level of the personality, people feel for organic analogies of this kind to describe an ongoing process — of which at times they themselves are as it were fascinated spectators: whatever next? "This awareness is always there but is gradually being unveiled as we become ready for each further stage." I am not sure how far any comment from me can add to these accounts, which may eventually convince by repetition but do not do much to explain what has happened — chiefly because this continuity through change remains as mysterious to the writers themselves as to anyone else. There is however one metaphor that is worth exploring a little further, not only because it is commonly used but also because it can lead to misunderstanding. This is the idea of a return.

I said earlier on that we were not dealing here with people who preferred to live in the past. The actual desire to go back to the thoughts and feelings of childhood for their own delight or comfort hardly occurs at all. What is more common is the notion of a return in the sense of a rediscovery of a truth once known and long hidden. As one correspondent puts it, the childhood experiences are all there, in all their vividness and immediacy, at the level of consciousness at which they were originally experienced. And there they must wait, to be reactivated when the whole personality has reached a state of development at which this can take place. This may only be possible when "I am ready to enter into certain experiences that will help to reactivate the earlier ones, thus making me consciously aware of them and of the link between what I experience now and what I experienced then as a child." This is not nostalgia. It is a recovery of something lost, a reintegration into an ongoing life of

44

something not treasured as a sentimental memory but found to have a new meaning, a new use. I quoted in Chapter 3 (pp. 35f.) a talk I had with a man who had described an intensely ecstatic moment in childhood, and his own reflections on what it had subsequently meant to him. He summed it up: "I am not one of those who still believe in God, but one who believes again, after a long intermission. It is probable that, but for that event in childhood, there would have been no 'again'." These are perspectives that only open up in the second half of life. (One of the great problems of religious education at the secondary level is that no-one is generally more remote from his childhood than the adolescent who is most conscious of having now put it behind him.) One man in his fifties observed how quite different his replies were now from anything he would have said twenty or thirty years before; another of the same age-group said: "I think that I am only now coming to know what it means to me to be a human being." Perhaps it is only with the spiritual maturity of old age that the true nature of the journey begins to become apparent: "I have reached the place", writes one, "at 69, where I know that it would be as easy to hold the sun in a teacup as fully to know and understand the all-powerful being we call God."

Marcel describes his sense of loss as he feels himself more and more cut off from "the mystery of my self". The very fact that he can consciously record this puts him alongside these others who like him feel the need continually to rediscover the child that they used to be. But why is it easier, as Marcel implies, for the poet? I went to see one of our correspondents — they must all remain anonymous so I cannot give you his name, but he is a poet of some distinction; and I quoted to him this remark of Marcel's. His comment was:

> I believe that poets, if they are to go on writing, must have something of the child in them, if only because for most of us the world as it becomes more familiar also becomes staler; one sees it "fade into the light of common day". But the poet I think can recover the delight and wonder, if he's still practising as a poet; in a common and dull object he sees something luminous and haunting. I must say that, when I practise this art or whatever you call it as a poet, I have to see what I'm writing about, the thing,

the object, the man, the situation, the scene that's beautiful or strange — it may not be beautiful, it may be frightening — but still I must see it with the freshness, the gloss with which the child sees it; and I would think this early event which stamped itself upon me so clearly is in this way a kind of root or stem for the later work I've written. It is a resource. One might say that recollection of it acts as a kind of tap-root, a shaft which sinks down to the spring of life.

Contrast this with an observation of André Malraux's, who observes in his autobiography:

Almost all the writers I know love their childhood: I hate mine. I have never really learnt to recreate myself, if to do so is to come to terms with that lonely half way house which we call life . . . I do not find myself very interesting.[4]

But however proudly he may rise superior to the nostalgia he despises in others, it cannot altogether be denied. A little later, he writes:

In the multifarious forms of that which drives us on, in all that I have seen of men's struggle against humiliation, and even in that sweetness which one can scarcely believe exists on this earth, life, like the gods of vanished religions, appears to me at times as if it were the libretto for some unknown music.

The song is lost; all that he is left with is the words.

To dissociate oneself entirely from one's childhood, then, may be equivalent almost to a loss of identity; though equally clearly, those who do, in Malraux's phrase, find themselves interesting, face temptations of a different kind: the backward look can be very fascinating. Remember what Marcel says about the danger for the artist who copies himself and may end up by stifling his own "special reality". The man who is to remain faithful to what Ben Morris in another context called "the child still active within"[5] must live out a paradox: he must be ready to turn his back on his own past if he is to rediscover his childhood.

This contradiction does enormously complicate such an inquiry as this. There are no simple answers to any question that is worth asking. For example, trying to cut my way through to the "bare facts", I asked our correspondents how far they could really separate their early religious feelings or ideas from the interpretation they later put on them. Could they distinguish between the feelings they had as a child and the meaning they subsequently gave them? The question proved well worth while. It clarified nothing, but it produced some very interesting answers. The analysis offered in the Appendix (p. 170) looks fine until it is realized that some people fall into the same category for exactly opposite reasons. The minority group, for example, who felt unable to make such a distinction, includes both those for whom these early memories can never be recalled intact (they have been "worn smooth by many tides of thought"; they "seem to belong to dream states in character: each is like a picture in a frame"; "what chasms of personal experience lie in between", and so on), and others who can make no distinction simply because these feelings have never changed: the sense of continuity is all. I do think it is worth noticing, though, that a clear majority, for whatever reason, felt confident that they could in their minds separate the feelings of childhood from any subsequent interpretation. To them there is no question of those original events having been obscured or covered up by later reflection or analysis; the memory of them is still clear and valid. (It is also interesting to note that the under 35s were more confident than the others that they could make a distinction, just as in answer to the previous question they had been more ready to give a higher value to their adult experience.)

But if the answers point to no simple conclusion (others may perhaps be more convinced by these figures than I am), the question prompted much illuminating discussion, often in the form of objections to my choice of words. What, for example, did I mean by "feeling"? "The feeling was completely real. As a child I did not interpret it, but I feel it was concerned with certainty, of a kind not to be analysed or reasoned about but simply to be accepted." Thus "real" feelings pass without distinction into "feelings of reality". Another protests against the way adults talk about religious feelings when all they mean is a kind of pious uplift, an essentially emotional self-indulgence that has nothing to do with the confrontation with reality that children experience — and adults too if they can "learn some kind of austerity towards these feelings". Others insist that meaning is not something discovered later by conscious

47

reflection: it may be integral to the feeling. "To me as a child experience and meaning arrived together." Or again:: "The strong feeling which characterized my experiences invariably was a feeling of meaning."[6] Statements of this kind will only raise problems for those who think of meaning in verbal terms. In that respect of course children are at a disadvantage, but it will not do simply on these grounds to claim that when once the original experience has been given verbal expression its meaning has been irreversibly translated, as though once conscious reflection has got to work we can never break through the verbalization barrier to re-experience the raw, uncontaminated feeling of the original. There can be a great wealth of meaning that is never put into words. The same is true of memory: we remember plenty of things we cannot describe. One correspondent talks of this reliving of childhood experience as "a somatic exercise rather than an activity of the brain", another of recapturing "the intense spine and gut responses" of those early days and with them the assurance that they were "a genuine contact with some kind of transcendental reality".

The problem I have been dealing with in this chapter, then, can be put in the form of two questions. What does it mean to keep in touch with, to be faithful to, one's childhood? And who is best able to tell the truth about it, the person who preserves the memory of it with detachment, or the one who is still deeply involved in what it meant for him? My own feelings I might express in another question. Do we learn more about the nature of a tadpole by preserving it in formalin, or by watching it grow into a frog? The analogy is inexact: the tadpole has no option, while the patterns that human childhood can take, the paths that its unfolding can follow, are infinitely variable. Still, that variety is always limited by a number of cultural and environmental factors. These we must now examine.

*   *   *

Further Examples

The clarity of childhood vision

The only aspect in which I think my childhood experience was more vivid than in later life was in my contact with nature. I seemed to have a more direct relationship with flowers, trees and animals, and there are certain particular occasions which I can still remember in which I was overcome by a great joy as I saw the first irises opening or picked daisies in the dew-covered lawn before breakfast. There seemed to be no barrier between the flowers and myself, and this was a source of unutterable delight. As I grew older I still had a great love of nature and liked to spend holidays in solitary places, particularly in the mountains, but this direct contact seemed to fade, and I was sad about it. I was not quite able to grasp something which was precious.

(F. 46)

My first remembered experience of the numinous occurred when I was barely three. I recall walking down a little cul-de-sac lane behind our house in Shropshire. The sun was shining, and as I walked along the dusty lane, I became acutely aware of the things around me. I noticed a group of dandelions on my left at the base of the stone wall. Most of them were in full bloom, their golden heads irradiated by the sun, and suddenly I was overcome by an extraordinary feeling of wonder and joy. It was as if I was part of the flowers, and stones, and dusty earth. I could feel the dandelions pulsating in the sunlight, and experienced a timeless unity with all life. It is quite impossible to express this in words, or to recall its intensity. All I know now is that I knew something profound and eternal then. Now I am deeply conscious that my human failings have taken me far from my childhood understanding of a greater reality.

(F. 44)

Childhood experiences were at a different level, on another plane, than those of later life. They were certainly more vivid, implicitly revealing; in a way surer, than later experiences; mainly different. Now that I think more deeply about them, these childhood experiences could perhaps be thought of as a reaching out to, a renewing of contact with, something my consciousness had been aware of before, now hidden from it. As I grew older these feelings diminished, and at no time did I connect them with religion, with the Church, or with a Christian God.

(F. 53)

My memories of my childhood are very very vivid and very clear to me. In the years from eighteen months of age to five or six all the foundations of my future life were laid. Colours were clearer, emotions were stronger, likes and dislikes more marked, life was rich with warm contentment. I am quite sure that all children have a clear awareness, almost like radar; and practically all children are far more aware of the emotions, feelings and inner conflicts in adults, in far greater depth than we give them credit for.

(F. 49)

The continuity of childhood

I have always felt the same. My awareness of that eternal hand was as clear to start with as it is now, it is no more now and no less.

(F. 46)

I do not feel that an earlier or later experience was more revealing; I rather feel each one had its time and place. I do not give too much importance to them in my life; by this I mean I do not find them unusual or to be separated from any of my life's experiences. It seems quite natural to me to have these. Yes, I rather suspect that they continue even as my awareness of life continues.

(F. 50)

In the final analysis the considering of the parts, which can have no being of their own, can in no way be integrated to form the reality of the whole, which is neither conceptual nor perceptual. So time and age are irrelevant.

(F. 65)

As regards early religious experiences being something from which one develops, I would be inclined to disagree. All religious experience is like something which occasionally breaks through the fog or density of materiality, and makes a kind of electrical contact. Sometimes one's own effort, one's own need is operative, but equally the light breaks through when one's attention seems not to be turned in that direction at all. I think over and above all one simply comes to the conclusion that there is another reality, dimly seen for the most part as through a fog, and also experienced in terms of inspiration, or on occasion revelation, when there is a quality of light, warmth, and a new depth of understanding, and joy over and above all.

(F. 59)

The growth of childhood

My childhood experiences were extremely vivid and significant and authentic. Those that I had as an adult were of the same kind in the sense that an apple follows apple blossom. They were not two different things. But the later things came after much thought and terrible anguish, and went much further, and meant a great deal more to me.

(F. 60)

The process of growing awareness is far from being an automatic process of growth like on the physical plane, but depends, according to my experience, on what part of us we nourish so as to link up with the abiding core of us, which is also the growing point.

(F. 56)

Full understanding I dare say is something few people achieve in this life, but I do know moments of serene assurance within myself which are like the opening flower of a formed bud that I have felt swelling in me since birth, and I sense the promise of its unknown future fruit.

(F. 29)

Like petals of a rose opening in beautiful order, my life has opened up bit by bit from that first clear and wonderful experience of God calling me by name when I was six and revealing his plan for my life. What followed was built on that first experience.

(F. 72)

I am more aware of a gradual process of growth without being able to pinpoint the stages; I feel that hidden within my child self were the religious ideas which very gradually unfolded; this process continues.

(F. 67)

I think I have been simply trying, in adult life, to grow towards the vision of childhood, and to comprehend more fully the significance of the light which was so interwoven into those early years. The original impact of light was so powerful that my inner world still reverberates with it. Later logic chopping, analysis and interpretation have in no way diminished the immediacy of that impact. Very importantly: this same consciousness of light has proved to be translatable as the light of common day living. In my own extremis, I have tried to remember the light and stand by it.

(F. 45)

I believe that the child has a wholeness. Looking back, it seems to me that I was whole in the sense that I was not yet disturbed by the sorrows that came later, at school. I was open, therefore, to receive. That simple wholeness is something like the wholeness of an animal, but more conscious perhaps. I would compare that simple wholeness with the more complex wholeness that you work towards slowly. I think I am much more whole today at 81 than I was at 40. And perhaps when a new wholeness has been achieved out of the complexities of life, one will be able to see the world invisible again.

(F. 81)

Travelling on; Travelling back

I do feel that life is a journey, a search, with religious discovery and deepening human understanding as one goes along, even if
"the end of all our exploring
Will be to arrive where we started

And know the place for the first time."
For me the pattern falls into stages of childhood to 12, secondary schooling, etc., then at 19 my parents separated. I shut all the hurts in a cupboard in my mind, and with them my awareness as mere imagination. I learned not to wallow in feelings. When what seems the worst happens you lose a lot of fears because you find that neither pain nor joy can remain at that intensity for any length of time, you just let it wash over you until it subsides. There were some years filling in time, the one religious development was the realisation what faith was — to know that God was there whether you believed in him or not. Then one day, two years ago, I was standing at the sink with a load of washing, when I had a vision — it was as if everything had a spirit inside, almost talking to you of the nature of it, of its essence. It was the atmosphere of "God walking in the garden in the cool of the day". For a moment I felt I could reach out and take it in my hands: "Hold infinity in the palm of your hand", but I could not. Then I recognised the pattern of the experience, felt mildly in childhood and forgotten — the longing not to be separated from it, the regret knowing it must be, the desolate loneliness coming away from it, the need for the comforting details of everyday life and human affection. I felt as one does on recovering from a severe illness or after having a baby, everything was fresh and new.

(F. 35)

I have had experiences in my childhood and youth which were quite mystical and vivid. As I have grown older, I no longer have these experiences. I may have enjoyed physical ecstasy as an adult, but as a young person I enjoyed spiritual ecstasy. My earliest feelings seem natural and right to me now. I was with the clouds of glory, utterly responsive to the wonders of creation, and a part of it. Probably the governess began to snarl this up. "There is a green hill far away" was the first thing I had to learn; sin and suffering. I had an awful feeling Jesus was not my man. I still feel I was never really young, except with my own intuitive perceptions before the age of five or six. Later, at thirty or so, and through psychic experience, I realised that the wrong kind of God was being taught. There followed a long and joyful period of self-repair and the effect was to get back to and start again from those very earliest feelings.

(M. 53)

I sometimes think that the curious sense one has in adult spiritual experience, that the reality has always been there but one had not noticed it, is due to the fact that it is a return to the far more vivid awareness of one's childhood perception. Certainly in childhood one is far more intensely aware of one's surroundings and of details, as one is in spiritual experience. I think we tend to lose this sensitivity and awareness as we grow older but that we can recover it through spiritual experience and also recollection, as Proust did.

(M. 63)

I feel puzzled at my earlier experiences. The thought of them returning is rather disturbing, but I see this as a possibility. I see them as a side of me that does not change with age, and which could always come through again if I let it. I certainly don't want to at the moment, in fact as I type this I can feel my heart beating faster.

(F. 23)

I am beginning to realise here as I write this that there have been four phases in my life in relation to God. The first phase, from the time as far back as I can remember to my early teens, that of knowing there was a God; the second phase of questioning, refusing to join the Church until I knew; the third phase, a blank period, followed by a time of believing but researching; and the fourth phase, finally, not just believing but knowing. My childhood experiences and feelings are comparable in depth and realisation to what I have found since; I felt that when I finally not only believed there was a God but knew, that I'd come in a complete circle; I realised that what I know and feel now was exactly the same as I have known and felt during the first sixteen years of my life. Though I did not have all the deep experiences, joys, sorrows, etc., of course that I experienced during my searching period. There is more wisdom and awareness in many a child than in many adults; it is the adults who lose this simplicity and don't bother to find it again that confuse and make life complex for the adolescents.

(F. 45)

I feel more and more how essential to any wider development and spiritual growth the early understanding of my own faith was, and is. It was the point of departure and like all points of departure still needs, for me anyhow, to be visited and relived from time to time, if the new understanding is to continue to emerge. "The road winds back but the road is not the same".

(F. 51)

Feeling and Meaning

The strong feeling which characterized my experiences invariably was a feeling of meaning. I felt myself, for a fleeting moment, to be part of a world of meaning, unrestricted by space/time and the limitations of my physical space-suit, part of a world where all was known, all was understood, all was acknowledged, appreciated, loved, with a love vastly transcending worldly concepts. Obviously I could not have put this into words, but the feeling was the same it is now, only the degree of introspection and erudition has changed.

I believe now that in my moments of religious experience I get through to a world of meaning which has objective reality, in fact more so than our physical world, and from which the possession of our physical body excludes us, temporarily. The world of meaning which I reached in childhood is the same world of meaning I can reach now more frequently and easily. The feeling of reverence, and release, is the same now as then.

(F. 50)

I remember what I thought of as "fizzy feelings": a diffused but aware excitement and anticipation of a wonder about to be manifested. I think I was reacting in much the same way as Richard Jefferies to the same stimuli. It was not so much meaning as content. These feelings were intensely life-enhancing — the effect similar to total involvement in some aspect of the arts — or being high on mescaline perhaps — it means I'm either sane because of it or potty and don't know it.

(F. 48)

The only early "religious" feelings which remain with me are those which have the same "taste" now as then — the feeling of wonder, joy, lightness and the paradox of not knowing *anything* and yet knowing for certain that "all was well".

(F. 55)

I can now, at last, fairly vividly recall the intense "spine and gut" responses to certain stimuli in early childhood. I cannot relive at first hand the intense ecstatic experiences of being of those days. But I can, in a sense, recapture them and enjoy them in my mind, with an assurance that they were a genuine contact with some kind of transcendent reality external to myself.

(M. 65)

In this description of feelings I have, of course, had to use interpretative language, as when speaking of the role of the unconscious in a nightmare, but I maintain that I can remember the feelings themselves, in the same sort of way that I can remember certain flavours in some foods that my deteriorating sense of taste no longer provides for me.

(M. 68)

I do not think I ever had any doubt as to the meaning of the experiences I had as a child. They were a sudden lifting into great joy, usually at the experience of beauty of some kind, in nature, music, poetry, etc. followed by a feeling of deprivation and "home sickness". Sometimes a feeling of great loneliness. These experiences are still with me, but I no longer feel so cut off and lonely. I think I feel a bit nearer to the source. I had a ten year period of "darkness" during which I hardly ever experienced the "joy" and the nearness, and felt I had lost it for ever. I suffered a great loneliness with no one with whom I could discuss things. But at the end it returned with greater intensity and variety. My childhood experiences are well described by Ruskin when he talks of "a continual perception of sanctity in the whole of nature — from the slightest thing to the vastest", and "I could only feel this perfectly when alone.".

(F. 67)

In relating or reliving the experiences I wrote about I try not to give meaning to them. I enter into the memory of these and strongly feel the experience. I am again the little girl, or the young woman, and feel what she felt, and remember the thought which came to her. It is quite vivid to me, I do not really attempt to understand or give meaning, the experience is complete in itself, I feel.

(F. 51)

The Experience beyond words

I don't find it in the least difficult or impossible to recall what it felt like to be a child, and I have often seen my early experiences being re-capitulated in my children, and the children I have taught. I think most people can recapture the *feeling* — what they can't do is to verbalise the meaning it had for them.

(F. 59)

I seem to be exceptional in that I have many very clear recollections (*not* induced by psychiatrists) from extreme infancy. Very many of these very early memories are of the frustrations of having no means with which to express myself, i.e. no language or only very elementary words. The lack of words does not affect the nature of the early experiences; I feel my memory of early religious experiences remains clear and valid now — and I am still suffering from a lack of adequate vocabulary to express these memories now: I never put a verbal interpretation on these experiences till in my twenties and so my early ideas did not get so distorted, and they were not so much in the nature of feelings but "knowings" through expansion of consciousness.

(F. 47)

I do not really feel that my memories of childhood are in any way clearer than those of adolescence, the twenties, or middle life — in a way I can almost travel back in thought to any part of my life that I happen to want to have another look at, and in a way do not feel that *essentially* I have changed much. Incidentally, one of my strongest feelings as a child was that of irritation at all the frustrations of *being* a child, together with the longing to grow up and realise my full potential in freedom. This feeling was so clear that it was almost as if I really had already known and could still remember what it was like to be fully adult. I think I have always had the idea that the essential "me" was timeless and free, and only for the present suffering all the inhibitions of being encased in a body. I am certain too that one's human awareness is, in some way, expanding and developing throughout one's life.

(F. 66)

In genuine religious experience one becomes intensely aware of

57

the utter inadequacy of words to express the new dimension of experience one is undergoing. "Feeling" is a totally inadequate word: it is far deeper than emotion. Nor is it mere thinking: it goes far beyond the intellect. It is a broadening of perception, transcending thought and feeling into a world where normal speech and thought do not apply. Words, after all, are a very crude method of communication. How could they be anything else? Mankind is probably only at the beginning of his spiritual development and words have been built on mainly mundane physical experience. Thus it is virtually impossible to describe one's childhood experiences. Poets and writers have attempted it with various success by the use of symbols and metaphors. But they can only communicate with those who recognise their experiences as similar to their own. Because a spiritual experience is so different from any other experience it cannot be distorted in memory though it may be incapable of description. I remember vividly what I felt but I may not be able to convey that memory to others. It was something "out of this world": it was a deep and abiding awareness, not intellectual, not emotional, a deep perception of reality.

(M. 65)

5

THE WEB OF HOME

"Born originals", said Edward Young, an eighteenth-century aesthetician, "how comes it to pass that we die copies?"[1] If we ask how far any written account or other expression of religious experience is influenced by upbringing or culture, the answer must be at every point. Influenced, that is, not determined. The choice remains ours; the range of forms from which we can select the expression that seems most apt is very wide; but it is the range offered by a particular language, a particular artistic or musical tradition and so on. Beyond that, in childhood at least, we cannot go. To this extent we are all "copies". Note that I speak of "expression"; the experience itself is another matter. One of the commonest features in these records is the insistence that fundamentally the experience was beyond description. What does this mean if not that, for that person at that moment, nothing in what he or she had been taught of language was adequate: that the experience at this point escaped the influences of culture. The truth of this is surely only underlined by those cases where people have rejected as inadequate the language that religion offers as appropriate. This conflict between experience and its expression runs through this and indeed any book that tries to reach the fundamentals of religious feeling. Sometimes though the two seem so perfectly complementary that we may not notice that they are two. When the expression is found entirely satisfying we may forget why this is so; we may even credit it with the creation of the feeling. When looking at the very earliest influences on the religious feelings and beliefs of children it is particularly easy to make this mistake. These accounts will put us right.

Not that too much weight should be given to the numbers (over a third of the men, rather less than that of the women; see Appendix, p. 161) who denied that they had been influenced in any such way by their parents or anyone else at home. All one can say is that they were not conscious of the debt. More is to be learnt from those who did admit influence. There are some delightful pictures of these early relationships, confident and unquestioned: "God was first in importance and my father came second, and everyone else way down the list. At the time I also thought that everyone else understood that this was the order of things"; the view of God "as he was portrayed in Morning Prayer" was the basis for "a very satisfactory view of life"; a happy, sheltered ambience, with or without grannies, nannies, holy aunts or evangelical housemaids, in which it was perfectly natural to include in your prayers "the entire Yorkshire cricket team, name by name, and my dog". To these correspondents, the web of home was a friendly, supportive structure, a secure base from which to look out on, and later to explore, the wider life beyond.

Almost equally numerous are those who acknowledge all this, but then find something to add. Parental religion, the ways of talking and thinking that came from church or school — this was one thing: "a kind of good manners like saying 'please' and 'thank you' "; such concepts were "no more than conventions which it was politic to subscribe to in order to be thought of as a nice child". But something more important was going on all the time at a quite different level. Ideas might be derived from parents, etc.; feelings were another matter. If you were lucky, conflict need never arise. Church could be accepted, it could even be fun; still, there was a suspicious resemblance between the prohibitions of 'Church-God' and those of parents. Besides He could be tested: "having directly challenged 'Church-God' one day by stamping my foot and swearing at Him (while in a furious temper at about the age of four) and then waiting for the skies to fall, and finding that they did not, I think my mind took on a new attitude; though continuing to be cautious, I ceased to be afraid of Him."

Real fears though remain; the capacity for wonder and for horror go together. When all is said about instability and deprivation and other factors of a disturbing environment, the world of a child is open to terrors which cannot be described in purely psychological terms, realities against which "please" and "thank you" offer no defence.

> As a child I was aware of no split in God, but it is clear now that I acknowledged two gods; both had authority, the first shaped my moral outlook but the second had the power. When I was between 6 and 10, after I had said my prayers at my mother's knee with real sincerity, and she had seen that the night-light worked, had kissed me and gone, I immediately lay flat on my back, folded my hands and prayed my real prayers, pouring my whole soul and body into the business. The object was, and it was a matter of great urgency, to include every created possibility, that is, to reach from one end of the scale the tiniest thing and at the other to stretch my mind to include the universe, of which I did have some primitive conception. "Oh God, please, please I pray with all the ants in the world and all the baby fish and the bird's eggs, the rivers and mountains, the sky, the stars, the planets, the sun and moon and the universe that I am not sick in the night and that an aeroplane doesn't fall on the bungalow, and I don't have leg-aches or bad dreams." I had no sense of sacrilege, of that I am sure, and I believe that I saw no difference between this God and "Our Father" whom I had addressed a few minutes earlier in quite different terms; but "Our Father" had not the same power to ward off my terrors.
>
> (F. 49)

Both these "gods" had "authority"; it was only on later reflection that the writer came to analyse the different strands in her thinking. If there were anomalies in the earlier mixture, they were unimportant; it was only when fully "operational" thinking got to work that they could, and had to be, sorted out. This is of course a typical development. All sorts of paradoxes and (to an adult mind) impossibilities can be tolerated and held in suspension in this original vision. This is what makes it so easy for us to be patronizing about it, or dismiss it as fantastical and childish.

This does not mean that the thinking of children is just an unstructured jumble of contradictions. Far from it. When it comes to value judgements and the truth of feeling, children often have a disturbingly acute eye for inconsistency or insincerity. "One learned to be careful what one told one's parents." Their attempts to explain away ideas of God as "a very nice and poetic way of explaining things, but just like a fairy tale" meet with silent embarrassment. We may take this for acceptance, but how wrong can we be? "I never spoke about my own ideas to her, out of a sense of shame, feeling that I knew who and how God was and she did not yet have that understanding." And another: "I felt embarrassed at what seemed her abysmal blindness and ignorance and felt sorry for her." These conflicts are particularly acute in the sphere of morality: I shall have more to say about this in Chapter 10. Any information or teaching that does not measure up to the often sublime awareness of the transcendent whole is liable just to be ignored, in a silence we may easily mistake for consent. We should often be amazed at the assurance of these statements: "I simply did not believe people who told me to the contrary, because I knew from experience that they were wrong." Inadequate views of God receive equally summary treatment: "I was absolutely convinced that this must be a lie about God", "this" being teaching about Hell Fire.

Then there are cases where these early searchings and longings are met not with opposition or dogmatic pronouncements but with indifference. They go underground, growing perhaps unnoticed, to emerge later in strange forms we may discuss as infantile or pagan, or just lying dormant, half-forgotten memories of something one knew once and now just, but only just, beyond recall. Nothing more may be remembered than the sense of having "being kept out of some wonderful secret". The seeds may germinate in the end; this is how we come to know that they were there all along. In such cases, to speak of religious ideas or feelings having been shaped by early environment, or having their origin in parental influences, can only be true in a quite negative sense. The web has come to be felt as a restriction rather than a support.

Yet when so much of all this, whether positive or negative, must be operating at a level below that of conscious thought, how can one ever be sure? Certainty may always be beyond us; all we can do is look sympathetically at all the evidence, and much of it suggests that a lot more may be going on in these early years than most of us ever thought possible.

Certainty is even more elusive when we try to assess how far children's first concepts of God are based on their experience of their parents. Here we run straight up against the Freudian double-bind. As John Bowker has pointed out, "the basic defect of Freud's theory of religion is not that it cannot possibly be right, but that it cannot possibly be wrong."[2] You don't care for the view that you derive your idea of God from what you saw in your father? No, you can't be expected to, but this only proves its truth. It is pointless to try to disprove the Freudian argument. However if one takes a dispassionate look at what a number of thoughtful and not unperceptive people have said on the matter, that theory looks pretty thin. A reductionist view of this kind may make life simpler for the man who holds it, but he has only himself to blame if he is ignored by people for whom life as they have known it has an infinitely richer and more complex texture.

Still there is some support for Freud even here. (I say "even here", because those who have valued their early experiences sufficiently highly to write to us about them will not generally be inclined to explain them away in psychological terms.) Some support, but not much. Less than a third of those questioned admitted that they in any way derived their idea of God from what they saw in their parents, and of this minority over half qualified that admission in some way or other. There were some to whom their parents were "the rock and anchor of all existence . . . all-wise, all-powerful, always there". For such, the concept of an omnipotent God could hardly exist independently. For Freud, though, God was not omnipotent; and for some of our correspondents too God emerged as a father-figure no more lovable or predictable than the very human beings who provided the model. In one interesting case (quoted at the end of this chapter; see p. 72) the actual father is so inadequate and

63

unattractive a figure, unlike other fathers to be seen around, that an imaginary father is invented with all the good qualities the real one lacked. Before long, not unnaturally, this ideal figure "became God". Other substitutes are sometimes found for parents who do not quite come up to the mark. This kind of thing is a matter of common observation, and will give the psychologist no trouble.

What is less easy to explain is the insistence of so many that, in the words of one, "God was more". Love, protection, order, justice — one might have one's first experience of these things from one's father and mother. But to go on to say that the figure of God is no more than a construct, bred by emotional identification out of the superego, by which the child's inadequate critical powers are exploited to impose a socially necessary authority figure — this is mere speculation, an academic game that can only be won by constant resource to the joker in the pack: the theory of repression. "These things my parents were to me; but God was more. There was always a feeling of expectancy, of something far better, finer, that was just beyond . . ." Besides, if parents themselves evidently conceived of God as a being wholly transcendent, far beyond humanity, why should a child be satisfied with a lower view? When a loved and respected father in all humility accepts his status as a miserable sinner, what is a child to think? "I did not relate the idea of god to my parents. They were kind, loving, calm people. God was awesome, a huge concept I could not quite grasp."

Then there are those who are quite ready to admit that that old father figure did have an all too human origin. God might well "look like my father but with cloud from the waist down"; but the really significant experiences — they had nothing to do with that God. "Our Father who art in Heaven" might shape the moral outlook, and provide an order to which one could conform without any great sense of conflict, while the real "power to ward off terrors" lay elsewhere. When that early sense of a *mysterium tremendum* makes itself so undeniably felt, there seems little point in arguing about the origin of the anthropomorphic figure. That form may or may not be owed to parental teaching or a human model: the content, the meaning it

64

was designed to hold, too often proves too much for it, overflowing or sometimes even destroying the mould.

* * *

Further Examples

Family Influences

My early idea of God from around the age of 3 years was that he, God, was my father's best friend. In fact I'm not so sure that I didn't believe that my father had had some hand in making the world; at any rate, God was first in importance and my father came second, and everyone else way down the list. At the time I also thought that every one else understood that this was the order of things. Whatever opinions my father expressed on whatever subject were approved of by God.

(F. 50)

My early religious ideas owed a great deal to the influence of my family. I don't think early religious ideas are necessarily laid down in "helpful" or "sympathetic" situations. In my own case I am sure they were compounded of the tension between puritan principles in my father and instinctive humanitarian responses in my mother, which meant that from my earliest years I had to think as well as feel. My religion was certainly formed in the tension between my father's life-denying and my mother's life-affirming brands.

(F. 60)

Neither my mother nor father attempted to explain or describe God to me. He was indescribable as far as I was concerned, a Creator. But I am sure my parents increased my sense of God's omnipotence and mystery by their own awe and reserve in discussing the subject.

(F. 23)

I think I owe my early religious ideas and feelings to the influence of my family to the extent that my parents were entirely upright. Goodness was assumed to be desirable of attainment, and honest behaviour to be normal . . . I remember particularly a great-aunt known to be very devout, of extreme sweetness of disposition; and a colleague of my father's who gave me the serious attention accorded to adults. It was easy to talk about God to both these people. However, the special experiences I had in this period, unheralded moments of beatitude and felicity, not caused by any incident, were, it seems to me now, separate from these influences, although the latter may have provided in part my receptivity to the outside. They invaded me unawares.

(M. 63)

I owe my early religious ideas entirely to the influence of my mother, my grandmother, and various rather holy aunts. Also to nannies with a simple, natural, country faith, but there was precious little sympathy, simply direction. I started at five to learn the catechism, but no one objected when I included in my prayers the entire Yorkshire Cricket Team, name by name, and my dog. I never saw God in my parents. I loved them, but I didn't much like God from the start, that is, the God I was given in Church or by the Bible. But even at five I was intensely aware of a oneness with all living creatures.

(F. 65)

My grandfather was a deeply religious man. The greatest influence he had upon me came from his way of facing death. He ended his days in Croydon away from his beloved country. One day he came back to his home at the age of 94 and said he wanted to live no longer. He bought two bags of bullseyes (this appealed to me) and two paperbacks (Westerns) and said "When these are finished I shall be dead". He wanted no mourning and received his grandchildren cheerfully in bed. His doctor did nothing to resuscitate him. He was allowed to die with dignity. He had absolute Faith in a future life.

(F. 56)

Other Influences

To me, all adults were "They", and although one didn't take all "They" said as Gospel, it was often wise to pretend that one did, otherwise parents, or God, that rather tiresome old man up in the sky, might see fit to punish one. Unfortunately there were very few sympathetic listeners among "Them"; discussions about religion weren't "done" in our circle. What a relief if would have been to say to someone "I hate God", "Jesus is a sissy", which I quite sincerely felt at times: it wasn't just revolt. I picked up a good many silly superstitions in the village or from the nannies or from nursemaids who looked after us in bewildering succession. Such matters could never be discussed with "Them" or further exciting contacts in the village would have been stopped. One learned very early to be careful what one told one's parents. In consequence of not being able to discuss what one felt with anyone I developed a rather inadequate idea of God. There was a constant stream of visitors at our home, including missionaries, special preachers and clergy of all kinds, many of whom wore aprons and gaiters. The Bishops were a particularly friendly lot, and I got quite fond of them. They stood for a way of life in which order and decency, wisdom and reliability prevailed, and were, at any rate when they stayed with us, kindly and humorous. In later life I wrote a verse about them:

> The bevy of Bishops I knew in my youth,
> Crozier, rochet and gem,
> Were really quite human to tell you the truth,
> And I learnt about living from them.

(F. 65)

Both my parents were believers but neither were apt to talk much about their beliefs, or to teach me directly. My first real apprehension of religion that I can recall came from the housemaid, Alice, who was an enthusiastic follower of the Salvation Army. She would teach us choruses which we sang all together — "Pull for the Shore, Sailor" . . . and it was with her one evening that I first got an idea of the immense and lonely blackness of the night, and the distance of the stars, hence a sense of the power and strangeness of God, for I don't think I ever questioned His existence.

(M. 39)

The Origins of ideas and feelings

My early religious ideas, i.e. in terms of formal concepts, of God, angels and so on, were derived from family, church and school. However, though I repeated these concepts automatically, a kind of good manners like saying Thank you and Please, I distinctly recall regarding such concepts as no more than conventions, which it was politic to subscribe to in order to be thought of as a nice child, or a good child. *Real* religious experience at that time lay in incidents of the Browning "Sunset Touch" variety, i.e. feelings of significance. I don't mean simply that I was significant, but that *all* of which I was a part was meaningful.

(M. 44)

Here I must separate ideas from feelings. From my parents and from society generally I accepted without question until the late teens an anthropomorphic God, and a divine Christ. These were inseparable from moral precepts. They also promised protection. God in particular was a great comfort. I could do nothing for starving animals and birds freezing on the branches, but God could. Every night I prayed for people, animals and birds, conscientiously enumerating all I could think of. This caused me much soul-searching and took a long time. Besides, I kept leaving something or somebody out. I was about 8 before I hit upon the solution: "Bless every living thing". I reckoned God would sort out the wicked Himself. God and Christ, however, were somewhere in the background, they were there so to speak. What I now see as my *real* religions feeling I used to call (but this only to myself; I never talked about it or mentioned it to anyone) "Purity". This was the word I used as a child. There is no word I can think of to describe this feeling. It is the coolness and texture and scent of stone, and wood, and water, the primroses; it is the movement and sound of birds, it is light playing among leaves, it is life pulsating in every living thing, from a spider to an elephant, from a blade of grass to a tulip tree. I do not know how I came by it.

(F. 53)

As I grew up in a country vicarage I think that most of my early religious ideas were influenced in two ways; firstly by the family interest in going to church, plus hearing the Bible read frequently and beautifully. The secondary and underlying influence was of the country itself, and the beauty of all natural things, from which, for me, for as long as I can remember, has flowed a power which has renewed, sustained and upheld me; something which I felt to be both nearer to me, and stronger, more real and more easily understandable than anything else. Church was fun, but I have a feeling that I was always aware that whatever sustained me was something far greater. I have a feeling now that, consciously, I scarcely connected God with my parents at all.

(F. 65)

Conflicts

I remember sitting in my mother's lap at the age of 5, while she affectionately explained that the idea of a God was a very nice and poetic way of explaining things, but just like a fairy tale. I felt embarrassed at what seemed abysmal blindness and ignorance and felt sorry for her.

(F. 64)

My first religious experience, or rather the beginning of my religious experience (because I feel it is a religious experience to be alive, so I cannot say "this is a religious experience, that is just an ordinary one") was a very tragic one. I must have been 4 years old; I was sitting on a little footstool next to my mother, who read to me from a children's Bible about Jesus. I had no contact with my mother, but I loved Jesus, and the more she told me about him, for his kindness, wisdom and patience, for his being a perfect man, grew every Sunday. I was unaware, as his disciples had been, of the signs of coming disaster. I was totally unprepared when suddenly my mother told me about the crucifixion and what led up to it. I fell into an abyss of sheer black desperation. My misery was such as I have never since encountered in my life — which by the way has had its fair share of happiness and despair. If I had at that age known that there existed the possibility of ending one's life, I would have committed suicide. Some days later my mother must have told me about the resurrection, but the blow had been too heavy for me to recover in so short a time. What some people think of as necessary for us to reach an understanding of another life going on around and above and within our everyday life, this was the severest misery to me. I started to distrust the Bible, and what I heard in church. And at a very early age I discovered a difference between the Old Testament Jahwe and the loving father that Jesus taught us of. I remember that, although I was very sensitive to my surroundings, I discovered that real happiness exists independently of life's situations, because there is in man an unchangeable, inextinguishable source of happiness, a link with the Universal Life. Although of course my emotions, my knowledge and my capacity for understanding have matured, I have the feeling that my religion of today, my feeling of Unity with all living beings, and above all the certainty of the all-pervading Life and Love from which no-one and nothing is excluded, is the logical outcome of a natural growth which began with this first desperate moment of truth when I was 4 years old.

(F. 41)

My mother did her best to give me an idea of God, and who will blame her for not succeeding? I never spoke about my own ideas to her, out of a sense of shame, feeling that I knew who and how God was and that she did not yet have that understanding. I had the feeling that my father, who did not speak at all about his ideas and emotions, knew what I knew and lived by that.

(F. 41)

Rejection

All this argument about whether God could create the world in a 6-day week struck me as being totally irrelevant, morality too, in its narrow "nursery" sense, while music, poetry and all forms of beauty leading to exaltation and self-transcendence seemed a natural part of religion, and I simply did not believe people who told me to the contrary, because I knew from experience that they were wrong.

(F. 41)

My first inner conviction, a pure feeling, belongs to my childhood. I had called my brother a fool, and my mother said: "He who calls his brother a fool is in danger of Hell Fire". I was so enraged to think that God could be unjust that I did not say my prayers to Him any longer, but to Jesus with a postscript: "N.B.

God, if this is a lie about you, then it is to you that I say my prayers and you will understand the situation without further explanation." I don't know how old I was, perhaps nine or ten. I soon felt absolutely convinced that this must be a lie about God, and that He was just and loving.

(F. 74)

I had heard from the pulpit that the unbeliever would go to Hell. I puzzled over it as a child, and then dismissed my doubts as heresy. Later the thought came to me "There is no one, however bad, I would wish to go to Hell. If God would do that, and I am so unwilling to see one soul cast into Hell, am I better than God?"I began to doubt the Bible, as not completely consisting of Truth.

(F. 57)

My mother was an atheist, my father an agnostic. I suppose we heard of Christianity when we went to school. Religious ideas came through books, the coloured fairy books, myths, legends of Greece and Rome, Tales of Norsemen, etc. Religious feelings came from beautiful surroundings, the cycle of seasons, animal life-cycles, looking at a speck of dust on a pond, and reflecting that inside oneself there was a centre of quietness to be built up like this in expanding concentric circles.

(F. 35)

I was brought up as a rationalist. I went to school and school prayers at five. I remember after repeating that not a sparrow falls to the ground without God knowing it being shown by my mother a sparrow caught by Lewis the Cat and being told that God had not taken care of that particular sparrow. I remember lying in bed listening to the carol singers coming nearer and nearer down the road with their strange and lovely tunes and feeling that, even with a Christmas stocking to unpack at crack of dawn and more presents, turkey and plum pudding to come, I was being kept out of some wonderful secret.

(F. 62)

God as Father: Father as God

I think my earliest ideas of God must have been derived from

71

what my parents were. They were the rock and anchor of all existence. They knew everything, were all-wise, all-powerful, always there. So what could God be but someone a little more powerful and wiser? Only he could not be seen. I think I must have been early teenage when I suddenly realised my parents were not all-wise, and not perfect, and that they could go away, or die; so God was not a super-parent.

(F. 66)

I think that my early ideas about God were drawn largely from certain characteristics in my parents. The idea of an impassive observer, rarely giving help or hindrance except at indefinite and often illogical times, very much like my parents.

(F. 23)

Yes, my early idea of God was derived from what I saw in my parents but it gave me a wrong idea of God, i.e. not as a God of love.

(F. 64)

My early idea of God related closely to my father; a rather distant and awe-inspiring figure who, we gathered, was on almost equal terms with the Deity, having incomprehensible interests in common.

(F. 65)

The Inadequate and the Ideal Father

I feel my early idea of God came directly from the contrast bewteen my father and the fathers of the few other children we knew. He was a stern, harsh character, while others seemed kind and gentle. He obviously hated all children, including his own, whereas other fathers showed love to their offspring. So I invented for myself an imaginary father who was all love, gentleness, kindness and justice. This father became so real to me that I began sooner or later to discuss everything with him and eventually to address my prayers to him. It seemed entirely normal and reasonable to me to tell him all that had happened during the day, and to be able to complain to him also when I had been unfairly treated. I can vividly remember that something in

72

me knew that I could not deceive this imaginary father: it would be no good telling him a falsehood or blaming anyone else for something I had done. He would know the truth. I do not know at exactly what point the imaginary father became God, but it would have been some time before I was 7 years old.

(F. 49)

Other Father-figures as God

God, I realised, to me had been modelled on my old godfather, the Rev. — —, vicar of a remote fishing village in Yorkshire. He never wore clerical attire except in church, and was something of a legend, even in his lifetime. It was said that he patrolled his parish on a Saturday night with a horsewhip, rounding up drunks and giving wife-beaters a bit of their own back. True or not, he was quite a character, and I enjoyed the annual visits to the vicarage which used to take place around Easter. I was very much privileged, being a god-child, by being taken to the study and questioned, gently but firmly, on the Catechism. The — s were not very well off; I remember very stale buns, but to me they were very special, coming, as it were, almost from the hand of God. He was quite a good model for a child's "The Lord". There was in addition to all else an aura of mystery about his home, which was reputed to be haunted, and contained a cuckoo clock which struck, it was said, as many as 22 times.

(F. 65)

God as an Extension of Parents

God was an extension (an added bonus) of the love and constancy of my parents.

(F. 49)

My earliest feeling of God was love, and this I understood because I received it from my parents. But God's love was more so. God was just, but more so. He was forgiving, everlasting, unselfish. He never deceived you, was never cruel, could be justifiably angry, could be disappointed in you, never lied to you, did not pity or scorn you, took care of you, did not expect more than your best, was happy with you and sad with you. These

73

things my parents were to me. But God was more. There was always a feeling of expectancy, of something far better, finer, that was just beyond . . .

(F. 60)

God as Wholly Other

From what I understood, my mother and grandmother who had our early education in hand believed that God was a being above them; that this being was ever present, invisible, or a spirit; that It was almighty, all powerful, and was called upon often, especially during times of stress, and was looked to for justice and help. He was a being to whom even my mother, father and grandmother were subject.

(F. 51)

I feel confident that I should have been amazed had anyone told me at an early age that I was conceiving of God in terms of my father. My father conceived of God in terms of a Father, and I absorbed this in the same way as his views on horses or strawberries.

(M. 60)

I do not think my early idea of God was derived at all from what I saw in my parents. God was, so I was given to understand, the great Creator of all things. Mysterious, wonderful, to be worshipped, obeyed and loved. He knew everything about everything. One could as well say that one got an idea of an elephant by looking at an ant.

(F. 67)

I remember very clearly from the years before I was nine listening very carefully to the words in the Litany and to the Responses of the Congregation, my father among them, and being very much awed by what seemed to me to be tremendous words. Everyone seemed to me to mean what they were saying. This being so, if my father could seriously call himself a miserable offender, and he was the kindest of men, how good did one really have to be to be satisfactory to God? I had no idea of God at all, at least not in the form of a person. Certainly I did not relate the idea of God to my parents. They were kind, loving, calm people. God was awesome, a huge concept I could not quite grasp.

(F. 53)

Not at all, I think; the love of God always seemed quite on a different plane from anything I saw in my family.

(F. 45)

Not at all. My father seemed either asleep or out.

(M. 33)

My idea of God was not derived from what I saw in my parents or in any other person. As a child I loved rambling in the countryside alone, and I always felt extremely happy and somehow in close communion with everything I saw around me. I remember very well trying to find out from books (which I avidly read) where the wild life originated from, who made them in the first place and for what purpose. Sometimes I sat in deep thought pondering over these things, and my parents told me not to be miserable. I knew that they did not understand, and I kept this wonderful feeling of communication with someone I could not see to myself.

(F. 49)

I did not connect my vague conception of God with what I saw in my parents: for a long time God was too vast a concept for me, he was way up there, far above everyone and everything.

(F. 68)

6

"LET 'X' EQUAL THE UNKNOWN"

"Certainty, of a kind not to be analysed or reasoned about but simply to be accepted." (p. 47) If anyone were to propose this as his aim in education to-day, his attitude would be thought mediaeval, or worse; and he would certainly be charged with indoctrination, which is just about the worst thing one can possibly be accused of these days. Yet education as we know it in the west has its roots in the church; for centuries it has been carried on in the name of religion, and religion, in this country at least, is the one subject in which by law our children are required to be instructed. What relation then do the kinds of experience and insight that I have been describing have to the schooling process? And what importance or relevance does the teaching profession see in them?

Not long ago I met a group of by no means inexperienced teachers on an in-service course and read them examples of the more deeply-felt accounts of childhood experience. Their reaction was merely to assure me that while these stories were very interesting the people who wrote them must be quite exceptional; their own pupils were not like that at all. What actual percentage of the school population of this country can record such experiences from childhood can only be guessed at, though studies like those of Michael Paffard suggest that the figure may well be higher than we might think.[1] A recent pilot survey in Nottingham also revealed an interesting fact: over 50% of a random sample recorded having at some time had some kind

76

of religious experience but almost all of these believed they were in a very small minority in this respect. The fact is that whether this kind of awareness is common or not it will never be suspected to occur at all by a profession whose view of childhood is limited by the type of educational psychology now prevalent. It will not be suspected because it is not expected; and expectations, especially in relationships with young children, can be immensely creative — or repressive.

"Nothing shall come of nothing", said King Lear to the daughter who, he thought, had not asked enough of him: "speak again." Where teachers cannot believe in the reality of this experience in their pupils, and in consequence expect nothing from them, nothing will indeed come back. Their low expectations are confirmed. That young people in our schools are now becoming increasingly bored with what is in consequence being offered to them is evident from the widespread malaise of indiscipline, absenteeism, falling academic standards and disruption. But this may also be a sign of hope: they may have had their bellyful of unreality.

In his book *Rumour of Angels* Peter Berger lists among his "signals of transcendence", those universal indications of man's discontent with mortality, the sense of the damnable. Our positive values may be blurred, but deep down we all feel that some things are just not on. Berger deliberately chooses to argue from an apparent negation rather than from a positive sense of justice because that would involve him in theories of natural law and so on. He is concerned, that is, not with a metaphysic of morals but with an irreducible feeling which will "stand out as a signal of transcendence over and above socio-historical relativities".[2] Equally irreducible, I suggest, is the hollow sense of unreality that must come over any clear-sighted observer of the way we live to-day. Our political leadership, our economic system, our press, our creeping bureaucracy, our established religion — how far do any of these really achieve what they profess to exist for? How far do they even try? A recent poll in the U.S.A. showed that two out of three of the population agreed that "over the past ten years this country's leaders have consistently lied to the people".[3] Disenchantment may not

77

have reached that pitch in this country, but among those who have not yet become inured to the artificialities and compromises (to use no shorter words) that most of us accept as natural to civilized life scepticism is on the increase. And surely this is a sign of health. The causes of boredom of course are not always creditable: bloody-mindedness cannot invariably be put down to some metaphysical malaise. But even if we ourselves occasionally have difficulty in formulating what we feel to be authentically real, perhaps we should find hope rather than discouragement in this widespread discontent with so much that is unreal in our present culture.

This disillusionment may set in early.

It must have been in my first few days at school. I was only about seven. I'd seen in the senior classroom on the blackboard an equation: x equals this or that, and y the other. And there was I in the bottom form struggling with letters as one thing and figures as another. Figures never made sense to me, but I could understand letters: they were for writing letters home and that kind of thing. And then suddenly on this blackboard there were letters and figures joined together. And x and y and z, the ones that were no use for writing with, were suddenly coming into their own. So I waited outside this classroom, very bravely (I was a rather timid soul), and I asked one of these huge fellows as he came out what x was; and he said, "Little man, x is the Unknown"; and he gave the "Unknown" a capital letter. And I was delighted; this was obviously what education was about. Grown-ups knew all about x, and that was why they were able to say things and not do them, and generally let you down the way they did, because they knew this sort of unknown thing called x. And I was all agog — until I was taught algebra. The day came, and I was absolutely quivering with excitement. Some great sort of revelation was going to come. Well, first of all the chap said "Let x equal the unknown", and I thought, "Ah, this is it". And then it gradually dawned on me that x was just an unknown number of apples, or gallons of water through a pipe; just a number, and you were back where you were. That was one of the great disillusionments of my education.

(M. 53)

How far do our correspondents support this unenthusiastic view of education? I asked them how far schooling had been a help or a hindrance in the development of their religious awareness. A majority reported that it had, on balance, been helpful rather than otherwise (see Appendix, p. 163). But those who are tempted to take comfort from these figures might bear two things in mind. First that the average age of these writers is in the middle fifties. If my particular aim had been to investigate a specific aspect of the present educational situation I should have gone about it rather differently. (As it is, the under 35s are notably more severe in their judgement than the older age-groups). But my concern is with the capacity of childhood for a certain type of experience, and the impact on it of our traditional form of education, which has in essence changed little in the past half-century. The second point is this. Any education that is reasonably efficient will implant its norms and values well enough to make a radical re-appraisal of them a difficult and slow process. There are signs that our own system is rapidly becoming less efficient in this respect. Even so, one may still expect from large numbers of people a tendency to accept an estimation of relative values to which their education has habituated them.

This is particularly true of the kind of experience I have been describing. "I do not connect any religious awareness with my school life, which was a happy, normal affair." Or again: "I cannot recall that school had any influence at all, religiously, on me; I was just a normal schoolgirl." These off-hand remarks give the game away so neatly that the point need not be laboured further. It really is a game, education I mean, and the sooner you learn the rules the easier life will be. "Schooling — teachers, books, the whole environment — seemed in a completely separate compartment from the development of my religious awareness." But trying to live at two levels only meant trouble. So "I deliberately inhibited the inner life and became highly scientific in outlook". The result was evidently, from the school's point of view, very successful. If our priorities in education reflect the needs of what is essentially a competitive society, the kind of competence that our schools will reward will be one that is just not compatible with that slowly maturing inner process which is the growth of religious awareness. "I would willingly have talked of the inner life, if the setting had seemed right," this correspondent concludes; "but it wasn't, and this didn't much concern me. I enjoyed school and learning very much." Not all children have the same flexibility of temperament. Those to whom compromises of this sort do not come so naturally find the conflict less easy to resolve: "the harshness, the indifference of my environment made me look to myself for a faith and belief I did not find outside." But within such a system good can be done by stealth. My favourite out of all these accounts tells how a little girl used to hide at unauthorised times in the library and only discovered years later that one teacher had known all along and had put out books specially for her. ("She remains a real friend of mine.")

At this point I must face the objection that the development of religious awareness is not the aim of education, not even of the subject "religious education". In the past it may well have been: in the days when the so-called "confessional" approach was still unquestioned teachers would not have been ashamed to hope that their pupils might become better Christians, more clearly aware of where their salvation lay. True, there may have been little more respect then than there is now for the personal experience of individual children. I do not myself regret the passing of what Gilbert Ryle used to call "the booming note" of those self-assured days.[4] But perhaps something has been lost when a professor of education can declare that "religious thinking is no different in mode from non-religious thinking"; it is no more than "thinking directed towards religion".[5] Stick to Goldman's formula and you will save yourself a lot of trouble. This spirit of clinical objectivity does in fact pervade much of current thinking about religious education. It has much to its credit. The phenomenological approach enables us all to look at religion, and religions, from a new angle. This can be refreshing. But this new objectivity, encouraging curiosity at the expense of involvement, does enable people to know a great deal about religion without really knowing what religion is about: without relating it, that is, to any personal experience, to what one correspondent calls "that deepest part of me which was always hidden from others who never suspected its existence".

There is of course such a thing as invasion of privacy, and this can be particularly offensive when attempted in the classroom. There are many things that children are happy to keep to themselves: "No-one understood, but that was unimportant." There are things that need silence and solitude: "an awareness that appeared to grow and intensify from being away from other people". The last thing I want to do is to lay down rules to cover all such situations. Take the little boy quoted earlier who was so excited at the thought that the algebraic "x" was going to be the key to all his aspirations. Whether I should have ever begun to be aware of the cause of that transcendent elation I have no idea, still less how I should have tried not to disappoint him. Crises of this sort no doubt pass daily unrecognized, when they should be the greatest challenges that teachers can ever face. Whether all that excitement is to be called religious is another matter, but was it any less so than the feelings of the little girl, quoted in the last chapter, that she was being "kept out of some wonderful secret"? There is of course a time for speech and a time for silence; but there is a world of difference between the silence of respect and the silence of indifference.

But I have not yet done justice to many positive points made in the replies to this question. Obviously there is a place for learning about religion, especially in our increasingly plural society. At the time it may not be appreciated. "Water off a duck's back", says one, but later "when I became religious it provided some sort of backlog of information and tradition". There is a good deal more of this kind of thing; teachers can take heart from it. In the name of efficiency the profession is no doubt right to lay more stress on aims and objectives in the classroom, and to require criteria for success or failure in achieving them. Frankly, though, I am sceptical of some of these formulas; in R.E. particularly we may so often do much better than we know. "Things stored in my sub-conscious enriched my religious awareness at a later period when I was ready for it." And then there is learning by heart, generally considered pretty old-fashioned today; it gets more than one appreciative mention. Perhaps we have lost our nerve too quickly over this. Not only can the memory be enriched with things recalled later with gratitude — "I had to learn Isaiah 53 at school but now it is *real*" — but words themselves can have an incantatory power that operates at a level deeper than any logic: "I got drunk on words: 'Ewigkeit du Donnerwort' ". Not all that is learnt then need be understood; in fact the effectiveness of an incantation depends to a great extent upon its *not* being understood. And then, most important of all, there are books.

Here what is recorded more commonly than anything else is the feeling of recognition. "In some poets and writers I recognized my own 'sense sublime' of 'a motion and a spirit that rolls through all things'." "I recognized it in myself as an old if unnamed conviction" — this of the mysticism of Hopkins, Wordsworth and Coleridge. A problem here incidentally is that no distinction is made in some of these accounts between childhood and the beginning of adolescence. Still, many make it clear that, while the "comfort from knowing that others had experienced these strange feelings" may have come later, those feelings themselves go back a long way; also that there is a continuity here that seems unaffected by age. Even the Bible, which we are constantly reminded is not a children's book, is found to "contain something that corresponded with my own earlier experience". But much more often it is through poetry, fairy stories, even science fiction — anything in fact that the imagination will respond to, that this feeling comes: the delighted discovery that "someone else had said what I had felt".

Arguing from silence is always questionable. Still it really is remarkable that so many of these writers talked appreciatively of what poetry and imaginative literature had meant for them, while of the other arts they have practically nothing to say. Music gets an occasional mention, though more often in connection with church than school; the visual arts hardly appear at all. Why not? Is it too much to point to the quite abysmal level of "visual aids" that so often grace the Sunday School or the RE classroom? I am not only thinking of William Hole, Heinrich Hofmann or Margaret Tarrant, those faded Medici prints or dog-eared Botticellis of a generation or more ago. Techniques have improved since then; colours are gayer and photographs more vivid; the social gospel at least gets a fair clout.[6] All the same I doubt if there is much more now to be seen in our schools than there ever was to stir that sense of mystery or move a child to that delight of recognition that comes so easily through poetry. The tradition of Christian sacred art has not been so rich, especially in the last three centuries, that we can afford to ignore the less explicitly religious painters and sculptors of our own day, when most so-called religious art is totally lifeless. A great many of our original correspondents do in fact emphasize how much they have come to owe to the visual arts. Here Van Gogh and Henry Moore rank alongside Michelangelo and Leonardo as seminal influences; distinctions between the sacred and the secular cease to matter. But all this comes later. Opportunities are surely being lost here. Our education is still predominantly verbal, and the non-verbal type, the natural visualizer, for whom the truth as well as the delight of the world will come most naturally through the senses, too often gravitates to the 'C' stream.

The priority we give to these verbal values is everywhere pervasive. It may also be seen in the severely functional logic of our contemporary school architecture. Some of this seems to me the ultimate expression in glass and concrete of something that goes back three centuries and more to Descartes and his pursuit of clear and distinct ideas. We should not of course be ungrateful: the buildings our new schools have replaced rarely evoke nostalgia. Still, something may have been lost. My last quotation in this chapter is from a correspondent who has been much involved in and has reflected deeply on the problems of education through much of a long life. In childhood she had had a visionary experience of unforgettable intensity in the meadows near her country home; "I saw through", she says, "into a beyond which I cannot describe apart from saying that the beauty of it was not of this world." She compares it to Traherne's early sense of the beauty of the earth. But this was before education had got to work.

> I suggest that this was able to happen because I was still whole with the simple wholeness of childhood, before my being was broken up into pieces at school, where I was unhappy at the transplant from the freedom and the beauty of the country round

83

my home. Many children would surely know this same kind of experience if they could have contact with the earth and green grass rather than cement.

(F. 81)

Experiences "of a kind not to be analysed or reasoned about" can clearly never "simply be accepted" as the basis for education, at least in its later stages. I am not arguing for the kind of irrationalism that sees nothing in any values that are not first "authenticated" by personal experience. What is sad is to see reason identified with a kind of dissociation, almost a kind of alienation, as though nothing but contamination could result from any imaginative identification with the object of study. This approach could conceivably be appropriate in the study of the cretaceous deposits of the miocene; with religion it could be different.

Further Examples

Companionship

From the age of 6-10 I was greatly influenced by a revered and loved form-mistress (who taught all subjects *except* religious instruction!), who gave a focus to my vague aspirations and led me to become aware of love at the heart of all relationships; she encouraged me to practise the presence of Christ's loving spirit, who was above all a friend of children, whom He understood better even than those closest to us, our parents. This was a great spur and comfort to me, for I felt myself, the deepest part of myself, not really understood by anyone, although I had a very loving relationship with my family. I now had someone I could share my deepest part with, which was always hidden from others, who never suspected its existence. It seems to me, looking back, that a bridge was built between the feeling and the thinking part when this idea took root, and it helped my development.

(F. 56)

Isolation: hindrance or help

"God is a spirit", etc., one of the most consoling thoughts given to me. There seemed to be a strange absence of people who could get me on with this idea. No-one understood my realization of something beyond the physical self.

(F. 70)

Schooling was of no help in my religious experiences. I do not remember learning much, apart from what I thought were boring details about some people's lives thousands of years ago. I have always felt an acute distaste for religion in church, or at school; I do not know why. I never felt close enough to anybody to discuss anything at all.

(F. 62)

I feel that all my education was a block and a barrier to real religious experience. It gave little help or guidance in "living", and was always wary of delving too deeply into mystery and crossing thresholds. I felt, particularly in adolescence, that my real self was neglected by the educational system and teachers, and that they were ignorant of fundamental truths. An education lacking in wisdom. As a child I longed to break free from rigid day to day round of lessons which I always felt stifling and often irrelevant.

(F. 23)

I do not think that, apart from poetry, which I adored, anything that I was taught at school had much, if any influence on my own natural and apparently inborn religious awareness, which on looking back at it now seems more like something deeply inherited and Celtic, because it appeared to grow and intensify almost entirely from being *away* from other people and by myself, either in the garden or the surrounding countryside. So that the line from Psalm 121, "I will lift up mine eyes to the hills, from whence cometh my help", has always meant something absolutely real to me.

(F. 64)

However ineffectual this teaching was, it had this saving grace: in its total failure to make Good Christians — or good anythings — of us, we were a little freer to become ourselves.

(F. 30)

School and the inner life

Schooling, teachers, books and general environment seemed in a completely separate compartment from my development of religious awareness — which was a personal matter between me and God, in my early view. I deliberately inhibited the inner life and became highly scientific in outlook, questioning my "hunches" at every turn, and learning to be silent about them. I would willingly have talked of the inner life, if the setting had seemed right; but it wasn't, and this didn't much concern me. I enjoyed school and learning very much.

(F. 43)

School was a hindrance in the development of religious awareness. I went to boarding school at the end of my ninth year, and I was most dreadfully hurt by the lack of love there. It made me afraid of human beings, and I have been afraid of them ever since. In spite of this I made a lot of friends and had a lot of fun, but it is a period of my life that I look upon mainly as a waste. My religion tended to get sentimental, except as far as Scripture lessons went — we always seemed to be doing St. Matthew's Gospel. It was the only subject over which I ever cheated: we unscrupulously cribbed from each other. It did not trouble my conscience then, and it has not done so since.

(F. 60)

The environment seemed mostly hostile to me and made me suffer. The schools we attended were poor and the teachers mostly indifferent. If my religious awareness was developing, and I believe it was, from the experiences I was having, the harshness, the indifference of my environment made me turn inwards, made me look to myself, for a faith and belief I did not find outside.

(F. 51)

The deep peace and happiness I felt was incredible. Often at the weekends while everyone else was watching television I would go to the bathroom or shut myself in the loo and open the window and talk to God, or this presence I had known, or all the many people that I could not see but knew were there . . . I remember kneeling on my bed and knowing that someone was kneeling beside me sharing it all with me. So really it was experiences like these that kept this alive, not so much school. School just quietly confirmed it through scripture lessons and matins and communion on Sundays.

(F. 18)

School and Nature

I turned to books increasingly for companionship, searching for expressions of experience similar to my own, both as to the beauty of the natural world, and my own sense of something beyond it, a timeless eternal "something" behind natural phenomena . . . Early in my teens I discovered Richard Jefferies, Henry Williamson and Traherne, and felt strong comfort from knowing that others — and adults — experienced these strange feelings, which I never mentioned to any person, though I have no idea why not. They seemed too precious and personal — a sort of talisman to be treasured in private.

(F. 58)

When I first had to study Pope's "Essay on Man" I was much struck with "Lo the poor Indian whose untutored mind saw God in clouds and heard Him in the wind", because I felt exactly like him and was more inclined to say "Lo poor Pope".

(F. 68)

Books

Schooling has had an important formative influence on me for the simple reason that it opened up the world of books, which played a fundamental part in my later religious development, when my mind was bent on seeking answers to fundamental questions. In retrospect I am convinced that the fairy tales, myths, legends and sagas I had absorbed in my earlier years were important in feeding the deepest part of me. Things expressed symbolically in fairy tales which were stored in my subconscious and enriched my religious awareness often at a much later period when I was ready for it.

(F. 56)

In general I felt that my schooling was a hindrance to the development of religious awareness. There were no teachers or classmates who ever related to the energy which caused the facts to exist; they would instruct me only with the rational facts. For this reason I much preferred books, as I could feed data into my own head at my own pace and interest, etc. I enjoyed imaginative lessons such as art, dancing or legends, stories, etc. as they seemed more relative to my feelings about the source of energy.

(F. 26)

I don't think I was much, if at all, influenced by the ordinary orthodox teaching at school. By far the strongest influence in my childhood was reading George MacDonald, particularly *The Back of the North Wind*, in which I think I recognized a truth already known in myself. I think these books and some fairy tales set a direction for my thinking from about 9 to 10 onwards.

(F. 65)

As far as religious instruction was concerned, it consisted largely of studying the journeys of St. Paul or The Book of Kings, and was very dull. But through literature I became aware of the mystical approach to religion and nature, and responded to it as my natural element. I do not think this mystical awareness — the inner knowing — was ever in conflict with the superimposed evangelical outlook. There was never any violent struggle or rejection, but the latter faded away as the deeper sense grew, because it came from within, and was not overlaid from without.

(F. 64)

Books have had far more effect, at least on my early development than people. From the age of 5 or 6 I scarcely ever had my nose out of a book. Many of these came from the school libraries, and by the age of ten I was pretty well versed in Greek, Roman and Norse mythology among other things, including Natural History; and my first introduction to Science Fiction came in a story of a Professor and two children who inadvertently drank something that made them so minutely small that they nearly drowned in a raindrop; and I found this adventure so moving that I think I then became aware of man's heroism in the face of quite insuperable odds, and the power in the microcosm.

(F. 30)

The Spell of Words

I was not affected by the morning hymns, they were just routine tunes. I heard better music at home. It was always the words, the Old and New Testaments, and Prayer Books. No revised version has the same hypnotic effect. In a sense they were incantations: "When the wicked man turneth away from his wickedness and doeth the thing that is right, then shall he save his soul alive." I didn't know what it really meant, but it was tremendous.

(F. 53)

There was a vast poster on the back of the WC door in an elderly relation's house which was fascinating: I learnt it by heart for the sonority of the words: BE STILL AND KNOW THAT I AM: GOD SPIRIT LIFE KNOWLEDGE POWER HOLINESS HEALTH WEALTH STRENGTH UNITY LOVE JOY PEACE OMNISCIENT OMNIPRESENT OMNIPOTENT and thou shalt worship NO OTHER GOD BUT ME. The doors in our house had Kipling's "If" and the Laws of the Navy which I liked better still. These tracts stood me in good stead later on when the meaning filtered through.

(F. 52)

Pictures

When I was given, at the age of about 10, Arthur Mee's Children's Bible, what really fixed my imagination were the pictures; these, printed in soft, mysterious browns and greens, were mainly Pre-Raphaelite evocations of Old and New Testament Dramas, many by Watts and Burne-Jones, and their effect was quite indescribable. They continue to strike the same chord in me — I can only describe it as a poignant and profound sense of significance, of their latent symbolism, of the beauty of Man's pain and promise. Then, of course, it was just an acute and pervasive feeling . . .

(F. 29)

Music

At all schools I sang, and this was all the joy I had out of Christianity. In the music in Choir and Prayers I could come to believe there was someone worth singing for, even if the words range false. So I sang for my half-discovered God.

(F. 29)

On all special occasions the choir would sing cantatas, such as *Elijah* and Stainer's *Crucifixion*. My earliest recollection of feeling the horror of the crucifixion was the music that accompanied one of these cantatas. There is a terrifying organ passage of deep, deep notes somewhere near a passage about "darkness covered the earth". Year after year I dreaded yet half yearned to hear it and feel again this unspeakable suffering and the unimaginable relief of "It is finished". I think it probably went back to 3 or 4 years of age, this sort of feeling without a name . . .

(F. 45)

7

CHURCH GOD

I have called this a study of the religious experience of childhood. The question of how much of what has been discussed so far is properly to be called religious is not perhaps all that important. But as I now propose to look at the impact of religion on childhood, and at influences that may reasonably be called religious, I cannot postpone the issue any longer. At any rate I can begin to clear the ground.

Note first that one can with some show of logic keep the word "religious" to be used in a purely limitative sense, strictly with reference to "religion". Thus we all know what is meant by a religious book, a religious person, religious music, even a dim religious light; no difficulty so far, provided of course that we all agree on our definition of religion. And here there will be no real problem if we confine ourselves to the conventional activity with which we are generally familiar, and regard other uses ("football is his religion") as derivative. So far so good. But what about religious feeling, or the religious spirit? Can these be defined purely in relation to the activity or the organization we know of as "religion"? One might as well set about discovering what is meant by the sporting spirit by looking at organized sport. It is not only historically that religious feeling and religious experience are prior to religion; they are at all times the fuel that keeps the flame of religion burning. So it is not by starting from the security of the familiar institution but by probing the mystery of an experience that may take unfamiliar and disturbing forms in every generation that we must explore this aspect of the religious. We must turn upside down Cicero's old dictum, that the wise man is the one who is no longer able to be taken by surprise.[1] Of Saint-Saens, the most learned French composer of his generation, it was said by Berlioz: "He knows everything; all that he lacks is inexperience". It is only by being constantly open to the unexpected that any tradition, religious or otherwise, can renew itself and stay alive.

The ambiguities of this word "religious" may lead to misunderstanding. Michael Argyle, for example, declares: "Women are more religious than men on all criteria".[2] His concern is with religious behaviour, and from all the evidence he adduces — tests of church attendance, the saying of prayers, expressions of belief — the conclusion follows. So it may come as a surprise to discover that recent sociological studies in this country and the U.S.A. indicate that religious experience, in the wide sense in which I use the phrase in this book, is equally commonly reported among men and women, with if anything a slight preponderance of positive responses from men.[3] It is true that of those who answered Sir Alister's original appeal women outnumber men by about two to one, but as I have said these writers are not necessarily representative of the population as a whole, and there are various other factors to be considered. In sending accounts of childhood experience women are in an even more marked majority; their accounts also show on the whole a greater sensitivity and attention to detail. None of this though should be held to support without further inquiry any general judgement on differences in religious experience between the sexes.

So we should not judge the "religious" in feeling or experience simply by reference to religion. But this does not mean that religion has nothing to offer in the nurturing, or indeed the initiation, of such experience. From the very beginning, as I have said, we are all to a great extent culture-bound. I am not forgetting those experiences mentioned earlier that are beyond words, when we seem to stand outside our culture, which is part at least of what ecstasy means. But if the vision of childhood is to be more than a flash of ecstatic illumination one of the things that keeps it alive will be tradition. By this I do not mean the passive acceptance of inherited concepts. One of the functions of a tradition is to provide a structure of ideas and forms of expression. These are not only a means of growth; they also offer something to react against. We may not be able to say what we want, but not this, not this at any price. The resulting conflict can be creative for the individual; it can also give the tradition a shot in the arm which will either reanimate or kill it. But that is only one aspect of tradition. More positively, it is the distilled wisdom of the past. Unexciting it may be at first sight: a brandy rather than a champagne, but like all essences powerful stuff, not to be taken neat and needing to be diluted with the fresh water of each new generation. Reaction against tradition may seem a necessary condition of life, but new growth must be very hardy to survive long without it. And often it is traditional religion itself that gives the first impetus to that growth.

What early memories do our correspondents record? "What I was made to attend as a child has become a joy, a privilege, a delight: the services of the church, infinitely rich and varied." But this has a suggestion of appreciation only in retrospect. What was actually felt at the time? "It felt good", says another, "to be part of a large worshipping community who acknowledged the presence of something greater than themselves." There is a good deal more of this kind of thing, and, though there are plenty of reservations expressed, those who have something positive to say are in the majority (see Appendix, pp. 164F.). For some it was the simple liturgy, the Book of Common Prayer, the Litany, "Cranmer's magnificent prose", that made "an indelible impression of reasoned goodness appealing to reason." Others remember the feelings roused by the rich pageantry of ritual, music and bells, the "ecstatic religious poetry" of the synagogue, "the beautiful, half-comprehended language", "the sonorous sound of intoned and sung Latin" and the sense of mystery to which all these contributed.

But the mystery itself? It will be protested that most religious services do not aim at anything so crude as giving people religious experiences. Such experiences do occur occasionally in church or synagogue; we have evidence of that, if it were needed.

More often what gives meaning to religion, even at an early age, is the same sense of recognition as I noted in the last chapter. A child may respond to religion as he responds to poetry. "The great festivals of the church quickened a sense of nostalgia in me, almost as if I had once known something which I had now lost." And again: "I remember some sense of something I could not identify . . . I can clearly remember even now it was nothing to do with liturgy, or atmosphere, or religiosity, but it was awesome." It is impossible in most cases to disentangle the different strands here: to say, that is, whether it was in religion that this feeling first found expression, or whether religion supported something already discovered elsewhere. In some the mystery of ritual helped to "strengthen a sense of awe and reverence with which I was familiar in nature"; others talk of "an awareness of happiness and awe and joy at just being there." What is important is that there was in so many cases this natural response to religion as something if not comprehensible at least not alien. Looking back on childhood people often find it hard to put their finger on any particular incidents or special moments when a corner was consciously turned; they can still be aware that a great deal was going on. "The source of comfort, forgiveness, love and healing was beginning to come through the organization."

Church then was often felt to be congenial; but was it necessary? Even more, it might be felt to be necessary, but was it sufficient? "I had a real love of the church, but it was never essential for my feeling for God;" "I loved the atmosphere, but nothing seemed to satisfy an inner need." Where something has been discovered independently of religion, that religion has a test to pass: it is judged by a truth that has an authenticity of its own. But not all children are so consciously critical. As with education, much is accepted without either enthusiasm or resistance, and is found to have been of value later on. However there is one field in which they are invariably sensitive and often disturbingly clear-sighted.

"It did not make sense to me that with one breath God told the Hebrews they were to love their neighbours as themselves and with the next told them to kill all the inhabitants of Canaanite

94

villages. I could not understand why it made sense to other people. When I was 8 I was taken to hear an evangelist who was holding services in our church. He described most graphically the flight of a soul to hell after death, and the fire and horror that sinful soul found there. For the next 14 years I had repeated nightmares in which God was trying to find me to throw me into hell and I frantically tried to find a place to hide from Him. To this day I can feel the terror these nightmares created in me. I hated God with my whole being.

(F. 73)

This acute sense of justice will come up again later. A religion that conflicts with it has no chance at all. There are other accounts of this intense reaction to hell-fire preaching. Evangelical Christianity in particular, with its obsessive insistence on a sense of sin as the key to morality, sometimes shows particular insensitivity to the feelings of children, though perhaps it does more harm in adolescence than in the earlier years. It is not that children do not need moral guidance, and they may be particularly open to such influence when very young. The conflicts set up by those who so clumsily exploit this apparent passivity without any awareness of the strength of feeling already there may take years to sort out. It is worth noting in this connection that one of the most traumatic incidents quoted at the end of chapter 5 ("My first religious experience . . .", p. 69) occurred to a little girl whose mother was a professionally trained Sunday-school teacher.

Children then have this quick sense of injustice, and with it goes a penetrating eye for insincerity or hypocrisy. "Churches seemed peopled by the listless, the fanatical or the ostentatious. Nobody seemed to mean what they said or sang; they went because they Ought To, or out of a superstitious unease, or for sentimental reasons. There was nothing wonderful." Here again what might be called the unreality principle is at work. Even where religion is felt to be sincere, or enjoyable, what had it got to do with the real world? I quoted earlier from Elkind's discussion of "the origins of religion in the child" (p. 20). For him, religion is to be included among those "social institutions" that "looked at from the point of view of the individual . . . afford ready-made solutions to the inevitable conflicts with social and physical reality which the individual encounters in his march through life". He writes without a trace of irony, unaware apparently of "the inevitable conflicts" aroused by any religion that offers "ready-made solutions" to the problems posed by individual experience, I have so far quoted little from those who reacted negatively to organized religion in all its forms. They were a minority, though a substantial one (over a quarter of the younger correspondents). But many are quite outspoken, and their rejection is often total. Religion may be accepted when it offers a language, a means of interpretation, for an awareness of something already sensed, however dimly, to be real; but when it is seen merely to be presenting ready-made solutions — no. "There seemed nothing in the church that bore any correspondence with my own experience". That alone, it is implied, is real; that alone is authentic.

I have more than once let fall a reference to the idea of authenticity. An experience is commonly called self-authenticating when it brings with it an assurance of its own reality: "the feeling was completely real". Experiences of this kind, however impossible it may be to communicate the nature of that reality, constitute, as we have seen, a test by which all others stand or fall: a diamond to cut the hardest steel. But there is another and even more personal kind of experience to which the word self-authenticating can be applied. Here the reality of which we are assured is not that of the experience itself, nor does it belong wholly to some transcendent order which somehow ratifies the validity of the experience. What is authenticated is the selfhood of the person to whom the experience comes: a rather different matter, it might seem. Yet when we ask what exactly it is that confers this secret and unquestionable sanction, its source is often no less mysterious and elusive than before. Religion may support this emergent self-awareness: it cannot dictate to it. No Church God can ultimately be acknowledged unless He is acceptable to this inner authority.

Further Examples

Church: Positive Views

As a small child the Sunday outing to Church was the most exciting activity of the week. The services always made a great impression on me, and I was terribly upset if I missed it. I remember sitting on my high chair singing happily for hours, copying the choirboys. I was quite certain of God as He was portrayed in Morning Prayer and found it a very satisfactory view of life.

(F. 58)

The words and language of the Bible and the Prayer Book mean a great deal to me now as in childhood. Forms and ceremonies, colourful vestments, incense, flowers and candles — all these influenced me deeply, positively then, and now. What I was made to attend as a child has become a joy, a privilege, a delight: the services of the church, infinitely rich and varied.

(F. 54)

In the parish church I was always listening carefully, thinking and pondering about what we were saying and having said to us. And the calm atmosphere no emotional appeals, no theatricality, a puritan approach even, made an indelible impression of reasoned goodness appealing to reason.

(F. 53)

The thing that mattered most was the morning service in the Book of Common Prayer. The Litany had a lasting effect on me, even though at the time it often bored me, and I diverted myself by letting everybody get well ahead and then starting to read at the beginning and seeing if I could catch up before the end.

(F. 60)

The Mystery of Ritual

The aesthetic appeal is what I remember as a positive influence

97

when I attended Roman Catholic services up to the age of 10. The beauty of the Cathedrals and Churches, the mystery of the ritual, the rich pageantry and above all the appeal of the glorious sound of music and even of church bells, all combined to strengthen a sense of awe and reverence which I was familiar with in nature. Although I was rather a solitary child, it felt good to be part of a large worshipping community who acknowledged the presence of something greater than themselves.

(F. 56)

I was certainly influenced by the services in the Synagogue. On High Holy Days there was an excellent choir; the music they sang in Hebrew used to stir me deeply, and the ecstatic religious poetry of the service filled me with an inner yearning. I often felt close to the mystery as a child in the Synagogue, perhaps partly because the whole ritual apparatus was so mysterious.

(F. 23)

Church worship was from my earliest recollection a time of great joy. The colour and feeling tone of the mass impressed me strongly, and I never wished to miss up to the age of 15. In those days the mass was said, entirely in Latin, but what one could not understand in the spoken word one received in the visual image, the acted ritual and the very sonorous sound of intoned and sung Latin.

(M. 55)

Church worship with its moments of mystery and the beautiful half-comprehended language used to summarise pain and fear, and express hope and reassurance: it evoked and nourished some fundamental response that no other area of experience catered for.

(F. 34)

Experience of Community

Church worship early on made me aware that you could have a different kind of spiritual experience when with others than when you tried to pray alone. I remember being rather shaken and dubious about what singing can do in a congregation. As I got older, I became increasingly disappointed and irritated during a mass when nothing happened between the priest and the congregation, partly because I had seen that something definitely could happen. My mother's family often said to me, even in my presence, that I would "get over" going to church, etc., and I was irritated to find myself growing critical of the institutional aspect of religion because I really wanted a kind of total permanent commitment, partly as a rebellion against the isolation of my family. I had wanted it to be my "society" where I would "belong".   (F. 38)

Conflicting feelings

Church worship in childhood was positive, not in terms of what was said or done, but by the fact that one was compelled, perhaps by the very boredom of the proceedings, to concentrate on the "sunset touches" one had felt. Despite my being a non-believer, in Christian or any other formal terms, I still feel significance when in church buildings.

(M. 44)

It was some years before I worked out that there was supposed to be a relation between church-going and religion. Or, if the former were "religion", then I did not have a word which meant "being-with-Him'. At all events, the two activities, to me, were as distinct as eating and going to the theatre. In fact, the simile is rather apt. I made a general distinction between the organized, socially-formulated religion and the spontaneous mysticism, philosophy and positive, willing evolution.

(M. 49)

Church worship was a duty. I went because it was the done thing. We had our own named pew in church and there we sat being good and looking properly respectable as the doctor's family. This had nothing to do with being with God, as far as I could see. Being with God happened out in the country, usually alone in glorious light, or, if in company, was generated by compassion and sympathy towards others. So I sang lustily, knelt when everyone else did, and longed to get home, change into old clothes, and go roaming in my beloved Herefordshire.

(F. 39)

I was influenced by religion to think of God as an awful parent, looking constantly to see what I was doing and condemning it anyway. "The eyes of the Lord are in every place, beholding the evil and the good". Since I expected constantly to be punished for my sins, I can't think how I ever got the idea that God had enough love in Him to help when I asked. As I usually had only God to talk to when troubled, I must have picked up an idea from somewhere that He would help me. Perhaps that idea is in all of us, without having to be implanted.

(F. 62)

I was influenced by sermons in the Church of Scotland: I was afraid of Hell. This influenced me. It was mitigated by my sense, feeling, awareness of God being loving. I think I half doubted Hell, but was afraid that it might be there. Anyhow that was teaching; the sense of a loving God was very deeply based, and did not depend on what was taught.

(F. 64)

The God I felt and knew inside me was separate from "organized religion" which seemed to be for Sunday mornings. The God I knew was for all the time.

(F. 45)

Sunday School I found distracting, confusing and upsetting generally. An over-earnest young Oxford undergraduate used to talk endlessly about someone called Jesus without whom nobody could get to God. Feeling as I did then that I knew God very well indeed, I could not see where anyone called Jesus fitted in, or that we needed him. I loathed the rollicking choruses "Build on the rock . . .", "You in your small corner. . ." What had these to do with God? I did not think of them as vulgar, as I do now, but I did think they were in some way unsuitable, unworthy. And I was repelled by the imagery: "Washed in the blood of the Lamb". I took this quite literally and thought it not only quite unpractical and out of keeping with keeping one's hands clean, but barbaric also.

(F. 49)

100

Church rejected

I was sent to Sunday School and later to Church (of England) each week, but found it tedious. My only strong memory of that period was thinking what a weak person Christ looked in the pictures; whereas I was sure he must have had a strong face. The "miserable sinner" aspect of orthodox religion had a large influence on my thinking between the ages of 5 and 9. I hated it, and felt more and more strongly that it somehow blasphemed against the beauty, light and all-embracing fusion of God, man and matter which I thought I saw all around me. To my shame, at the age of 9, I leapt up in the Church service, unable to bear the "for there is no health in us" intoning any longer, and shouted that God wasn't like that at all: that he was nearer than one's own hand. And I was hustled out in floods of tears. I was thoroughly shaken at having made a public scene and begged not to be sent to Church again. My mother, while not comprehending my distress, allowed regular Churchgoing to end at this point.

(F. 43)

My experience of Sunday School was quite irrelevant to the subsequent growth of my spiritual awareness, which has been totally personal and sprang originally from an acute sense of beauty in life, and the need to realise its meaning in relation to the apparent brevity of human existence. There was nothing wonderful in church. There was only the music — and in that music I found all the things they had never explained about Christianity. There were pieces that moved me to tears. But the Church that commissioned them left me cold, and I revolted against it.

(F. 30)

I think it is true to say that I was, and am, essentially "religious" in spite of church "worship" or other forms of organized religion.

(F. 62)

8

"MY OWN SPECIAL REALITY"

Authenticity: Lionel Trilling has recently pointed out that it is from its use in the museum and the sale room that this word has come to be part, as he says, of the "moral slang" of our day.[1] A work of art, that is, is authentic if it is genuine, if it is what it purports to be, if it is not a fake; if it is the real thing. So my feelings are authentic if they come from some genuine source, if they really represent the true "me". What may make them, or indeed my whole life, inauthentic is, first and foremost, society, which forces us all, consciously or otherwise, to conform, to compromise, to lead lives that are not in any genuine sense our own. So runs the argument; it goes back to Rousseau. The final state is one that we have recently learnt to decry in our search for a rediscovery of the self and a way of living in the world that we can call "authentic". "Cant" would perhaps be more apt than "slang"; still there *is* something wrong in the way we talk of authenticity, if only because there are implications in it that we do not recognize, or will not admit. How, for example, can we be so sure of the existence of that real, authentic, nominative "I", of which this pathetic "me", the object of so many social pressures and disabling circumstances, is only a poor imitation? Trilling goes on to criticize that school of contemporary psychoanalysis that finds in the unconscious, and in the recognition and fulfilment of its demands, a means to the recovery of authenticity. The target is an easy one. All the same this instinct to grope beyond the limits of individual consciousness for an understanding of the true potential of the self is a pretty universal one. There will always be some who see nothing more in this search for a personal authenticity than an attempt to justify self-gratification under the name of psychological fulfilment. But there is more to it than that.

"In the coming world", said Rabbi Zusya of Hanipol in the old Hasidic story, "they will not ask me 'Why were you not Moses?' They will ask me 'Why were you not Zusya?' "[2] The idea of a unique and personal destiny which each one of us is created to fulfil is common to many religious traditions. And we cannot, it seems to me, justify the use of this word "authentic" of our own lives unless we have some such idea to back it: a concept of a pattern or purpose specific to each individual life. There is something very old-fashioned in the idea of destiny; it has dusty associations with an authoritarian deity, and it is confused with fate. As for the latter, Buber makes the distinction well: "Destiny is not a dome pressed tightly down on the world of men; no one meets it but he who went out from freedom." Fate is quite different: "The only thing that can become fate for a man is belief in fate . . . To be freed from belief that there is no freedom is indeed to be free."[3] And if the authoritarian overtones are too strong, by all means find another word if you can. But it must not be one free from any suggestion of obligation. To be "authentic" means not just to be real; it means to be true to some other reality, to be in relation to this what one ought to be. And to be "inauthentic" is not just to be a copy; it is to be bogus. An apple tree which is sold to me as a Cox's Orange should not produce fruit that is large, green and sour; if it does, it is not an authentic Cox; it is not true to type. But what is an authentic man? Unless we regard them as "beyond freedom and dignity", men and women have a claim to be judged as individuals, not merely as members of a species.

I have already said something about Piaget and his great services to our educational system. Not the least of these, I suggested, has been the creation of a structure of psychological theory: a structure which can not only be used as the basis of professional examinations, but is also universally applicable in any "educational" situation. (And if you question why I put "educational" in quotes, I would ask in reply whether we are not more and more inclined to restrict this word "educational" to those situations or activities to which the Piagetian criteria of learning apply.) In a text book of educational psychology whose author and title I have mercifully forgotten I once came upon the observation, as a comment on a table of statistics, that "for the purpose of this study, children are regarded as more alike than they are different". The attitude is a parody of all that Piaget stands for. Yet what is the value of a psychology that does not concentrate on the predictable, the universal, the essential "alikeness" of all human beings? Writing in 1939 in America it was not only the experience of Nazi Germany that Otto Rank had in mind when he observed that all our educational systems rest on the assumption of a basic homogeneity. "Supported by a seemingly universal psychology of human behaviour, politicians and educators felt justified in molding and shaping the undefined masses according to their own purposes and ideals . . . Since men are not alike and cannot actually be equal, psychology could at least explain them as alike with the more or less open purpose of making them alike . . . As the expression of the mentality of a certain type it perpetuates this very type, hence, can finally be conveniently used to explain it."[4] Psychology has of course its part to play in enabling the individual to discover his own potentiality. But as Pascal said of the reason, its last step must be to recognize that there are many things that lie beyond it. "Man is born beyond psychology", wrote Rank, "and he dies beyond it, but he can *live* beyond it only through vital experience of his own."[5] The italics are his.

What then is this "vital experience of his own"? What is this personal authenticity, this "mystery of my self" to which I am to be faithful? Terms such as these are in fact rarely used even by adults. Nevertheless the feelings and convictions represented by these words are a natural part of the vision of the world of childhood. No prompting was needed for this kind of thing:

> Religious experience: I first became aware of this at the age of 3. In fact it made up the very first conscious thinking I ever did. There were two elements to it: (a) a feeling that I was in the

world to do certain things, that I had been sent here to carry out these tasks, together with an awareness that I didn't yet know exactly what it was I was supposed to do and that I would first have to find out. I was convinced that sooner or later the "call" to do the right thing would come (it hasn't so far). (b) A "knowledge" that I had come from somewhere before I was born, and that I would one day return to that somewhere. My preoccupation with trying to find out where I had come from was strongest during my earliest years. Later I stopped thinking about it, and I haven't yet started thinking about the "somewhere" I'm going to after death. But as a very young child I had a very strong and distinct feeling that my life hadn't started at birth, and of being frightfully old. Both these feelings were on my mind throughout childhood, and only really began to recede during a period of acute poverty as a grown-up. I'm still, at the back of my mind, looking for that "something". But as I get older and gradually give up most of the things I hoped to do in life, my little "something" is turning into something I have to find, rather than something I have to do. (F. 31)

One of the problems of such a study as this is that its subject is one that cannot properly be described except as a seamless whole, and here I am taking this or that aspect in turn, and dealing with each on its own like items on a laundry list. Childhood experience, in its widest sense, extends in time, not as a stone thrown into water sends out ripples but, as I have said, like a growing organism. Thus of the two main elements in this last account, written at the age of 31, who can say how they will appear in relation to the whole in, say, another thirty years' time? Clearly there is much still going on here, and this will often be so with the emergence of self-consciousness. The process may be slow and almost imperceptible, without identifiable turning points. One correspondent quoted Elizabeth Jennings:

Something is growing;
Watch it how you will,
Still you can never say the second
When the petals pushed to independent life.

But it does not always take this gradual form. Many of those who originally wrote to us identified particular moments of awareness. An inquiry about these in my questionnaire brought

105

in many more accounts of this kind of experience, often from the very earliest years of life.

To some this may come as a surprise. We know a good deal about the "crisis of identity" faced by the growing adolescent as he or she makes the transition from childhood to adulthood and becomes aware within himself of new powers and responsibilities. No-one would deny that this is a significant stage in the development of self-consciousness and independence. Its importance has been recognized in all cultures (except perhaps our own to-day) by ceremonial "rites of passage" which have emphasized the new view now taken of him by the adult society which thus accepts him as full member. But it would be a mistake to give a disproportionate significance to this particular transition. If we are to believe our records here, crises of no less importance for growth may occur at any time, both before and after adolescence; and particularly before. The crisis of adolescence is easy to identify: it is marked by unmistakable physical changes. With these changes comes a new potential of reflection and self-consciousness, so that now for the first time the emerging person can become fully aware of what is happening to him, and can make that awareness explicit both to himself and others. It is thus impossible to overlook. Adults may take little notice of earlier signs of development or transformation, but find these less easy to ignore. Adolescence comes as a challenge to them; both for their own sakes and for the sake of the new arrival, peace must be made. The relationship cannot be allowed to develop into an unhealthy rivalry, so it has to be recognised by formal ceremony (as in the past) or (as to-day) by private treaty. The latter is often embarrassing and less than satisfactory. But it is clear that there are other crises.

Growth may seem gradual and uncomplicated, and "normal" enough, but there may be many significant moments of truth, as well as much turmoil and resentment that we never get to know about simply because it never reaches the level of explicit expression. "No adult can suffer as a child suffers", writes one correspondent. Why? because adults can reason and analyse, relate this to that, see things in proportion and so on. This is neither prevention nor cure for suffering. On the whole, though, we learn to cope with life, to face what can be faced and to repress what cannot — and call this maturity. The sky of childhood is so quickly clouded over by what adults see as trivia that what lies deeper may never be noticed. They will get over it, we say, and regard as signs of immaturity the child's inability to react "sensibly" to everyday problems and disappointments, as well perhaps as those profounder questionings that we are no better able to come to terms with than they are (more often we have just stopped trying).

This restless and often traumatic search for identity, then, may be as characteristic of childhood as it is generally thought to be of adolescence. True, this is not a statement that can be regarded as proved on this evidence. Though it was made clear that the questionnaire as a whole referred to childhood, no specific age-limits were mentioned. In consequence, of those who replied positively only rather more than half described incidents occurring up to the age of 11. So the figures in the Appendix, p. 167, do not at first convey any very clear impression. It might at first seem significant, from the fairly even spread of records of this kind of experience over the span of childhood and adolescence, that no significant peaks appear between the ages of 5 and 15. But these questions were sent to a picked group who had made some mention of significant experience in childhood. If I had been making a study of adolescent experience and had chosen correspondents with this in mind, a somewhat different pattern of figures might well have resulted. One would expect there to be *some* differences between the kind of self-awareness that may emerge at, say, 16 and that which appears at 6. It may well be that the sort of brief account which in most cases is all we have is not precise or full enough to bring these out. I can only say that I could put many a childhood account alongside an adolescent one, and it would be very hard to say at what age each experience had occurred.

Self-consciousness, then: what does it mean? The vision of childhood, I have said, cannot properly be considered as strictly limited in time; it also extends in what might be called spiritual space. "As though the sky fitted the earth and the earth the sky"; the material simile stands for an even more mysterious unity. To become conscious of one's self one has at the same time to become aware of what is not the self. And to this not-self there are no limits. Studies of infant behaviour may indicate how the range of individual perceptible objects is gradually extended. These observations do not necessarily conflict with this other sense, described by one correspondent as occurring in moments of "extreme awareness" which had "a kind of intensified particularity"; she goes on to speak of "a realization of self and the whole in relation to oneself and out of time". Another frequently recorded element is the sense of being "part of something greater than myself". In some cases it may amount almost to a feeling of the loss of self. "In the real world", says one, "I have no 'self'; I am the things on which I pour my love. That is how it is now, and how it was when I was a child, though then I could not analyse the way I felt." Both dependence and independence are stressed in these early experiences, sometimes simultaneously. Paradoxes abound, as in the account quoted on p. 13: "I was at the same time so insignificant as to be almost non-existent and so important that without me the whole could not reach fulfilment." But this only appears self-contradictory when we apply the analytical language of adult logic to ideas and feelings conceived in an altogether different way; a point I have already made.

The self and that which is not the self: awareness may start with the body. "The realization came over me: 'my body is now that of a child, but it's not ME'." And again: "Looking at my naked very small body in the bath I thought 'how odd that I shall inhabit this for all the time I am alive'." This feeling is strengthened by actual out-of-the-body experiences, which may begin early. The discovery that there is more to the self than its physical embodiment may be the first experience of transcendence. Limits previously taken for granted are found to be unreal. In many of these experiences, in fact, there is an instantaneous leap from the sense of "me" to the limitless awareness of the infinities of time and space. "I suddenly felt old and aware of being somebody very ancient, weighed by Time; of almost unbeginning individuality." Some of our correspondents go much further than this, and describe experiences of "far memory", intimations of what led Wordsworth to believe in immortality: moments, as one insists, "of re-affirmation rather than awakening." Accounts of this kind will perhaps only be convincing to those who have had some such inklings of their own. The sense of belonging to a whole that stretched in time both before and after — this is much more common. It involves not only a curiosity about the "before": "Here am I, a little boy of seven; I wonder where I was eight years ago"; it also brings a child up against the fact of death.

It sounds morbid to say that the awareness of death is important in childhood. Children are certainly very much concerned with the subject: it came up frequently before I specifically asked about it, and I shall have more to say about it in the next chapter. But this interest is generally unclouded by the guilt and sentimentality that so often gets attached to it in later life. The discovery of death may be frightening; but sometimes it comes as a solution and a positively satisfying one. When it first comes home to a child that the real self is not confined to the body, that it may reach out to "all the things on which I pour my love", and that the door of eternity is already open, then death stands not for frustration or annihilation but for liberation. At present we are confined to what one body can see and do at one time and in one place: very cramping, when there is such an infinity of things to explore and knowledge to assimilate. But this state of affairs will not last for ever; one day the butterfly will ease its way out of the chrysalis and take wing and the whole universe will be at our disposal. "I felt that at the moment of death all these limitations would crumble round us like the walls of a prison and we should break free and cry out joyfully, 'Oh, I see!' Everything would fall into place and we should understand the purpose of the pain and frustrations of this life."

Within this perspective of eternity — they do not of course always use such solemn language — comes the sense of the reality of the individual, with a purpose and responsibility of his or her own. Death in fact gives a shape to life. It is premature in most cases to speak of an actual sense of destiny: this may develop later out of these childhood stirrings. It may start with no more than an inarticulate sense of urgency: "a strong sense of having only a limited time here — and how terrible it would be to reach the end realising I had lived my life on the wrong lines."

The discovery of the self, then, whether sudden or slow, may involve a great deal more than simple self-consciousness. (But when was that ever simple?) Was such an experience, I asked, associated with any religious feelings? Not a very intelligent question, perhaps. About half said yes; but it was clear that some said no only because they associated "religious" with "religion". Some also said their experience had led them to the rejection of "religion" as they knew it. When I become aware of being just my self, and at the same time of "the perfection that lies outside everything to do with everyday life", the language of the Sunday School may seem a little inadequate. But how important are words here anyway? Can these things ever be communicated? What really matters is to recognize that the experience, the search for "my own special reality", is not confined to any particular stage of mental development, but is a characteristic of childhood at any age.

Further Examples

Early Crises of Identity

Very early, at least from that painful 9-10 year time, I felt myself very much an individual, responsible for my sisters, aware morbidly that I must be "different". I think the self-consciousness was probably rooted in the religious awareness that I was impelled to feel by my unhappiness. No adult can suffer as a child suffers, because an adult can reason, understand, explain, escape. I suffered early and sought explanations early.

(F. 56)

The years from 8 to 11 I remember as pretty agonising. I was afraid of death, and of life for that matter, and subject to severe panic attacks which nobody seemed to notice. I couldn't explain them at that age of course, but looking back I don't really think they were caused by any mental instability but simply by my having reached a religious crisis at a ridiculously early age, and being quite unable to cope with it.

(F. 21)

I must have been well under the age of three. I remember distinctly being aware of thinking how silly grown-ups were not to understand, and I was also conscious of playing up to them and trying to conform to the image they had of me, or they projected into me (clever girl, funny child, etc.). I felt myself distinct from them, separated by their lack of insight that there was far more of me than what they saw in me, the undeveloped child part.

(F. 56)

I remember when aged 4 I thought the doctor and my mother were being horribly patronising, and I bit the thermometer to pay them back. At aged 7 I hated the doctor and my mother for forcing me to have my tonsils out on the kitchen table because I thought I should have been consulted.

(F. 49)

Perfection as Infinite

We were walking home along the pavement. I became spontaneously aware that each step I took decreased the way between me and my destination by precisely the same amount as it increased the distance between me and my point of departure. I had not sufficient command of language to tell anyone. It was perhaps the most thrilling and significant thing that has ever happened to me. It was a knowledge. I knew it was me. You see, I become bogged down even now as the recall comes over me for perhaps the thousandth time. For years I tried to put it into words. Help was impossible. If I had been able to ask what I wanted, that is, how to express it, there would have been no need to express it. It went with me wherever I went. There was something there to do with perfection, a perfect conjunction of increasing and decreasing. I see now it cannot be communicated — the perfection of it. And when I was 15, the formulation came, in a history lesson, and I let out a great shout of joy, and was duly reprimanded. But, as I recall it, I am three or four, and inarticulate, and can feel only the perfection that lies outside everything to do with ordinary life. No one understood when I told them in the lesson; "Can't you see! Can't you see!" I repeated helplessly.

(F. 50)

Far Memory: Reaffirmation

We had to start school on the day we were 3 years of age. I can remember that soon after this I would toddle off to school trying to recall that lovely place where I was before I came to this drab place with its rows of lower middle class terrace 6-roomed houses. "I don't belong here". I had filmy memories that I could not pin down of an atmosphere that was radiant and luminous, smiling and gracious. When, later on, I read Wordsworth's "Intimations" I knew precisely what he meant by "apparell'd in celestial light, the glory and the freshness of a dream". In a few years, alas, I also knew what he meant by "the things which I have seen I now can see no more" and "the man perceives it die away and fade into the light of common day." Wordsworth connected this radiant beauty with Earth and Nature, "meadow, grove and stream". As far as I can remember my mental processes, this radiant graciousness was nothing to do with anything "here". I

112

doubt if these thoughts and feelings were in any way connected with religion. Had I been asked about this and had I had the vocabulary and ability to formulate it I would have said they were above, beyond and at the back of all this drab earthly business.

(M. 73)

Particular Moments

I recall several "moments" in childhood. I see these now as flashes of self-consciousness (consciousness of the true self). It was a sense of otherness rather than of freedom or responsibility. It was not associated with religion, but rather with such strange moments as sitting in a barber's shop at the age of 7 and seeing the back of my head reflected in the mirror in front of me and a further reflection of my face and so on. If I am not clear, let me add that there were two lines of mirrors, one on either side of the shop. I can visualize this experience today, 62 years later.

(M. 69)

As a very young child (under school age) and occasionally later, I experienced periods of extreme awareness which I won't attempt to describe, except to say that they have a kind of intensified particularity — and a realisation of self and the whole in relation to oneself and out of time. I am now convinced that my earlier insights do, in fact, relate to a Reality — or God — and that this awareness is common, in some ways, to everyone.

(F. 46)

Self-consciousness as Absorption

Yes, I can recall experiences of individuation, but I cannot recall the first such feeling. I recall as a child (about 8) throwing myself on my back in the grass and feeling that I was spinning round with and was part of the globe. No sense of responsibility was involved, more the realisation that one existed as oneself, paradoxically because one was part of all. Formal religion in church terms was quite separate from this experience.

(M. 44)

I cannot agree with you that emerging into self-consciousness means to feel yourself as an individual being. On the contrary, you seem to lose your individuality and to dissolve into something far greater and wider that includes all individuals.

(F. 42)

I remember instances in my childhood when I felt a unity with the world around me verging on mystical experience. I did not at first associate such feelings with religion. They were usually the result of a deep realisation of beauty in nature or music. They were not so much a sense of self-consciousness as of absorption in something far greater than myself of which I was at the same time a part and glad and grateful to be so; an overwhelming sense of trust and gratitude to the world for letting me be a part of it. This was later amplified and deepened in periods of genuine spiritual experience when I and the world seemed to dissolve into a new and vastly more significant reality which had hitherto been only vaguely sensed but suddenly seemed to be revealed completely, so that one had the sense that it had always been there but that one had been unaware of it. Probably the first experience of this intensity of awareness came to me when I was a child of about 4 or 5 as I played on the terrace of our house in Sussex one early morning in summer and looked out over the mist-filled valleys and woods into the distance.

(M. 63)

Consciousness of the body

Yes, I can remember at six years old sitting in the sun on a compost heap in a cottage garden and seeing myself "as a dressed body in which I was", and thinking that I was "me" in a strange place and yet I was all right in the religious sense of being in an ordered universe. It's very difficult to put that into a child's words, but the glow of assurance has lasted against much disillusionment and through states of disbelief.

(F. 49)

I can remember being self-conscious from a very early age and feeling older than my physical body.

(F. 39)

When I was about 10 I had a strange experience which I still remember quite clearly. I was walking back from school and suddenly stood still as the realisation came over me, "My body is now that of a child — but it's not ME. Soon I shall have the body of a young girl and later of a woman — but it still won't be ME; I am apart from my body and always will be."

(F. 76)

Consciousness of Time as Infinite

During the year when I was 8 another important event happened to me. As I stood dressed to go out on one of those interminable and awful walks through the country lanes, I was actually thinking and considering my position, something like this — "Here am I, a little boy of seven; I wonder where I was eight years ago". At that tremendous thought I stood rooted to the carpet (remember I was alone in the room), with a wave of tremendous feeling sweeping over me. I suddenly felt old and aware of being somebody very ancient, weighed by Time, of almost unbeginning individuality. Eight years ago, thought I, why not eighty or eight hundred? I felt ancient and old and full of Time. Nowadays, of course, I cannot find the wording to state clearly what I mean. I remember it quite exactly, nevertheless.

(M. 75)

These experiences were not moral experiences but rather a feeling of intense awareness as though I had passed out of time, discovered a great all-embracing secret, become one with the world or — more exactly — as though the world were existing through me: I am myself — I am here — coalescing into one intense moment. I remember this happening some time in a field before I went to school and again on my seventh birthday. I have had similar experiences since, but more rarely.

(F. 46)

What could it possibly mean to live "for ever and ever" and "world without end"? Lying on my bed during the daily rest before lunch I would try to grapple with this idea. It was before my 9th birthday because I was still in the night-nursery of the farmhouse. It was also in that night-nursery, when I was only four, that I had that sudden and surprising realisation that I had only been in the world for four years. I can remember thinking (or feeling?) that four years was no time at all. I am certain that this thought had not been put into my mind by my parents. I can

115

remember it vividly as a sudden surprising realisation.

(F. 64)

Re-affirmation

I was born with this feeling of self-consciousness, as I only ever remember having moments of re-affirmation rather than awakening. These moments of affirmation were and are associated with a tremendous rush of energy throughout my entire body, causing me to feel a sort of warm vibrating glow within and without — total happiness and, above all, protection. They occur without rational explanation.

(F. 27)

1.
I was under a year old — unable to talk or walk. I was crawling on the floor and sat up to listen to a record that was being played on the gramophone. (I later identified the record; it was Segovia playing the tremolo study by Tarrega on the guitar). I went into a trance state but much of it I remembered after. In trance I "touched Heaven" — I became aware of an absolute totality and the magnificence of the ordering power — also a complete oneness. I was God and Totality in that instant and knew all. As I came out of the trance I was acutely aware of myself as an isolated part of the total that I had just been aware of. This trance is probably the greatest single experience of my life. It is extraordinarily difficult to describe and probably only lasted for seconds.

2.
This was close in time to No. 1, probably at about 15 months old. I was standing uncertainly and clutching the table-leg for support! Again this was a very brief experience. I got a comprehension of the all-controlling being, and the nature of the Heaven (or whatever you like to call it) that I had come from before birth. It was attractive and comprehensible. I was feeling unhappy, and I was shown in a flash my whole life in front of me. I was given the choice: I could die now and go back to the Heaven that I knew, or I could go through with my life. I chose the life in the knowledge that there would be another life to replace this one if I had chosen to die. On making the choice, my comprehension of Heaven vanished, but I remembered that I had

116

known what it was like; I also remembered that I had seen all my life, but that too vanished; but I do remember that, though my future was all planned out, the whole point was how I chose to react to it. I was also aware that this was the natural rotation. The Heavenly state was more desirable, earth-life being something of a penance!

(F. 47)

Self-Consciousness and Death

I kept bumping up against my own limitations. We could be only in one place at one time, listen to one thing or one person, and we had to stop doing interesting things to eat or sleep — lovely things to do but not to be forced into doing by a wearying body. I felt that at the moment of death all these limitations would crumble round us like the walls of a prison and we should break free and cry out joyfully "Oh I see!", and everything would fall into place and we should understand the purpose of the pain and frustrations of this life.

(F. 55)

The Awareness of Death

I can remember a vivid experience of self-consciousness when I cut my hand very badly (about 7-9 years) and it suddenly dawned on me that I was an entity that could easily be damaged in such a way that no "magic" could put things back to the original "perfection", and even that I could be snuffed out completely. I had a terrible horror of death.

(F. 56)

Before the age of 6 I was in terror of eternity, that endless floating around and around in space. Death became a nightmare. A child once quoted to me at that time "world without end". I was shaken to the core and had no-one to help me.

(F. 65)

Yes. I realised I was individual "me" when I was about seven; and at about the same time I understood that one day I would die. I was very shocked with the idea, I remember, but after worrying about it for a while I learnt to live with it.

(M. 52)

117

The Sense of Purpose

Both vision and light gave me, even then, a sense of there being a great purpose and significance within the universe which — while far exceeding my own small part in it and truly having no direct personal bearing on me — yet gave meaning to my own small personal life of that time, and has done ever since.

(F. 43)

I must have been no more than about five years of age when, having heard of someone who had died, I asked my mother why the person had had to die. I remember my shock of horror when she told me that we all had to die some day; it meant that I too must die, and there was no escape. She must have seen this, for she tried to reassure me: it wouldn't be for a long time, and when good people died they went to heaven, etc. But the awesomeness of death remained with me. One element in the impetus within me to search for ultimate meaning in life was a strong sense of having only a limited time here — and how terrible it would be to reach the end realizing I had lived my life on the wrong lines.

(M. 57)

The Sense of Individual Responsibility

I had this strong sense when I was a baby in arms. Naturally I don't know how old I was — perhaps 1 to 2. I was screaming and being carried downstairs (I remember which part of the stair) to my parents as being very naughty, or as not stopping screaming. I suddenly had this feeling of what I should now call emerging into self-consciousness. It was a sense that I need not scream, that I could choose not to. It was in my power to do this. It was a wonderful feeling, like what I'd now say was a religious sense. It was as if I could not help screaming before, had no choice in the matter, as if screaming happened to one, but then I feel that I decided. This was not associated with any religious ideas or feelings. I had none of course at that age.

(F. 76)

9

DEATH

The subject of children's ideas and feelings about death needs a book to itself. Any thorough study, for example, must consider separately a child's thought about his own death and those prompted by the death of others. Then again, much of the distress caused by the thought of death can be explained on purely psychological grounds, in the dread of separation or some other source of insecurity. There is also the question of what death actually means, what the content of the idea is, to a child. How does he first come to distinguish between things that are dead and those that are live? This whole question of infantile "animism" has of course been explored by Piaget, and Silvia Anthony has done further interesting work in this field. She concludes that "the child shows no concern about death before he reaches the stage of question about reasons, causes, motives and necessary connections between events".[1] Really? "No concern about death"? The material given at the end of the chapter hardly bears this out, and there is much more evidence I could have offered. It is only fair though to quote her subsequent qualification: "We have certainly found that during the early stages of language and concept learning children's notions of death may be limited; generalization is unsound, for these limited concepts have a great variety of content."[2] They do indeed. Studies of this kind are no doubt valuable to those who are interested in the development of verbal skills, and are happy to consider concepts as one thing and feelings as another — a pretty artificial proceeding, for, as Miss Anthony concedes, "there is no warrant for supposing that inadequacy of the concept ensures its emotional insulation."

From many points of view, then, what I have to offer here will be inadequate as a study of children's attitudes to death. I only bring the subject in here because these attitudes do often tell us a great deal about the world-view of childhood. This is why I give more space to records of positive feelings of acceptance or assurance, wonder or awe, though these are no more numerous than those of disturbance or fear (see Appendix, p. 168). (Besides, the latter are more susceptible of a psychological explanation). Some of these more negative accounts, though, are revealing in their own way.

If self-awareness, as I have said, may involve awareness of an infinite potential in time, both before and after this physical life, what about death? If it is merely the means of passing from one form of existence to another, very well. But what if it is the end, not just of this but of all life? "Total nothing for ever and ever and ever." To face such absolute extinction, to think that one day one may totally cease to exist — the thought is all the more disturbing to one whose sense of existence is so vast and infinitely mysterious. The child in whom this sense has not yet faded has so much more to lose than the adult whose perspectives may have narrowed, or who has come to terms with a "commonsense" view of life.

> Life to be sure is nothing much to lose;
> But young men think it is, and we were young.

Housman may have written better than he knew. However, most of those who recall their horror at their first thought of the inevitability of death seem to have had in mind no more than the end of physical life on earth. And to many this was something of no immediate concern: "it was something that happened to old or very ill people: all I had to do was to keep young and well". In other cases the fear of separation and isolation are clearly evident: "I begged my father to promise me that he'd live for a hundred years." Nevertheless it would be wrong to think only in terms of human relationships and their loss. There is often an irreducible element of protest, of "rage against the dying of the light". Death was the negation of something known to be real, so real that for it to be totally destroyed just did not make sense. "I felt outraged by death, furious at it." So some of these attitudes to death that seem negative are not so at all; rather they reflect an affirmative world-picture in which death seems an anomaly. To adults it is that picture itself that often seems anomalous, and so when we come to look at the positive attitudes that children take towards death we cannot always be sure what to make of them. "When a child I used to hold my breath to try to die for a moment because I was so intensely curious about Heaven." It is almost impossible for us not to be patronizing about such remarks. Our picture of heaven is no doubt tarnished; how deeply anyway did adults ever believe in this tinsel-and-kitsch eschatology that they handed out to children? How far can we really think ourselves back into that happy acceptance of death as a release into fuller life that seems genuinely to come quite naturally to many young children? "Death for myself couldn't happen and if it did was unimportant as I would always continue."

The ways in which children show up the hypocrisy of adults and their attitudes to death is often entertaining — or disturbing: it depends whose side you are on. The gap between what we really believe and what we think appropriate to the sensitivity or understanding of children is revealed in a glaring light by many of these accounts. Some are pure comedy: "I must have been about five when my mother felt she should enlighten me about death. She was at her most embarrassing when enlightening us about anything." Other cases are more serious. The self-absorption of adult grief may be seen as ridiculous and false; "Death meant people in black saying 'shush', and the biggest bell in the church tolling for hours. It meant suffering for the living when they wanted the dead person back with them for their own selfish reasons. I never felt sorry for the dead". Even worse is the silence and mystification with which we see fit to surround the whole business: "It was the unutterable black emptiness of everything . . . Night and day one seemed to be swallowed up in this inconsolable grief and loss . . . I seemed to drown and stifle in it." There are some pretty gruesome passages here, exposing nakedly the morbid behaviour of supposedly religious men and women when faced with death; they also illustrate the deep disturbance to children that can result when adults do not feel able to share their beliefs or feelings with them. Anyway, what can they say? Nothing could be more ridiculous than the assumption (which most of us tacitly act upon) that there is something about death that adults know and children cannot be expected to understand. The opposite is no less likely to be true.

Dead bodies, for example. Some children admittedly are disturbed at the thought of physical decay, but much more common seems to be a robust acceptance of the body as an essentially disposable container. One remarkable account describes the feelings of a child of six left with a baby-sitter who took her and her small brother to the public morgue. The sight of all the corpses propped up round the walls roused nothing but curiosity, which they proceeded to satisfy in the obvious way until they were told to stop. "We were told these were dead people, but it meant nothing to us." The misguided taboos by which their elders feel they must protect children may in fact rob them of a very satisfying experience. "I felt very peaceful and was fascinated by the corpse. She (a grandmother) was very beautiful: all her wrinkles had gone;" Another grannie "had very definitely gone and left behind a mask, like the cases grubs left behind when they became butterflies".

Death in fact is seen as part of a natural process, almost as evidence in itself of continuity rather than of a break in the cycle. This sense of permanence through change is occasionally enhanced by the kind of "far memory" that gives another dimension to self-consciousness, that "realisation of self and the whole in relation to oneself and out of time" that I mentioned in the previous chapter. This feeling of "reaffirmation rather than awakening" gives a new perspective to the idea of death. Some write quite explicitly about this: "During my first ten years death was simply linked with 'that other place' from where I had come." Others write equally simply about the exciting thought of "a return to something one understood and knew". How common this feeling is in the very first years of life we can probably never assess. Perhaps it is "screen memories" of this kind that give that extraordinary confidence to these early childhood views of death as not an end but a new beginning. These are summed up by one who writes: "My view of death never came out of a negation of life, but on the contrary out of its utmost assertion." How does any child come to trust life that far? When all has been said about the security given by a loving environment, and the influence, conscious or not, of a religious upbringing, there remains something irreducible that these factors do not touch.

This is not to say that the early influence of religion may not be powerful. Sometimes it can be unhelpful: "The Church's teaching about being in the grave 'until the last trumpet shall sound' haunted me all my life", says one correspondent. But as some of the examples quoted show, traditional teaching about Heaven and the after life meet a ready response and give great comfort. The question I would ask, however, is how far all these ideas would take root if there were not already some dim awareness, "something one understood and knew" to which they corresponded. How otherwise do we account for this quiet acceptance of a mystery not lightly to be spoken of, perhaps not to be spoken of at all? "Death seemed to me great and wonderful — 'eloquent and mighty' would have done well had I known the phrase". Mysterious, but unquestionably real; and real not just in the sense of universal and inevitable but because it related to something more real than life itself. "Little man, x is the unknown factor." That was no joke at the time, however hard we find it to enter into all that it meant to a boy of 7. As another correspondent put it, "Death seemed the only subject which realted to IT in any way. I knew that IT could not die as IT could only go back to where IT came from; which is no death at all." As we have already seen in Chapter 7, where religious teaching and, even more, religious ritual relates to an 'IT' with which a child is already familiar at some level of consciousness, it can evoke a resonance that can be both satisfying and enriching: the ceremony will play out an inner drama whose plot is not wholly alien to his experience.

Further Examples

Death as something to be feared

I had a terrible horror of death that I couldn't mention to anyone;
it was like a gaping black hole that I desperately tried to shy away
from, but unsuccessfully. Whether it was a religious experience in
childhood I can't say, but it grew into one later.

(F. 56)

Yes, vividly. I was eleven. I was horribly haunted for perhaps a
month with the terrible inevitability of death. If I touched myself
or any person I was conscious of the bones under the skin, the
skull under the face. It was intense and continual suffering.
Finally I got over it.

(F. 55)

I can remember when I was about 5 thinking of death when lying
in bed trying to go to sleep. I knew what death meant —
termination of existence on earth — and I was afraid. The
thought that one day I would die appalled me.

(M. 21)

A lady in the village died when I was 8. Night after night I cried
and was too frightened to sleep. Mum sat with me and told me
that it wouldn't happen for a long, long time and that when I grew
very old I would be tired and glad to rest. But I didn't believe her.
I knew time had a way of catching up with you. It passed.

(F. 25)

My grandmother died when I was about 9. About this time it
dawned on me that everyone would die and I used to say little
prayers (usually when I was in the lavatory): "Please God don't
let any of us ever die". But I really knew we would.

(F. 58)

When I was nearly 5 years old I would often cry bitterly at night,
particularly when it was bellringing practice night, at the
realization that some day my parents would die, and indeed the

overwhelming knowledge that everything in the world would die some day. I found it an absolutely terrifying thought. I can still remember the feeling of utter desolation. Although I knew then that there was a life after death I was always so afraid that there would be a journey, a long, dark journey and people would perhaps get lost or too tired before they found Jesus.

(F. 51)

Total rejection was an early reaction. Death seemed too awful to contemplate. For instance I can't remember when I was first aware that I had no mother, but I could never believe that I would NEVER see or know her, and all my life I have had, as a result, a horror of, for instance, saying the unforgivable thing, or doing the irrevocable act, death I suppose being in my mind as the ultimate in finality and something one could never change, storm, pray, rage or whatever, and thus, nothing could ever be the same again and anything of a like character was to be avoided at all costs.

(F. 49)

Conflicts with adult attitudes

When I was 4 years 9 months old my father died. Mother cried uncontrollably. I can remember crying too and friends would say, "Poor child is overtired and should be in bed earlier". There were no words to explain that it was not overtiredness, it was the unutterable black emptiness of everything and everywhere: night and day one seemed to be swallowed up in this inconsolable grief and loss. It was like an invisible aura round her and I seemed to drown and stifle in it. My father's name was seldom mentioned because he was dead, and this seemed to make it worse. A sort of taboo lay on any reference to him, although we had to keep going to his grave in the cemetery and putting chrysanthemums on it every Sunday. One part of me found this morbid grief unreasonable, because my father was supposed to have gone to be with Jesus in Heaven where everybody was happy and all their questions were answered. If this spirit was in Heaven, I could never quite see why we had to go and put flowers on his grave where his body was slowly turning to a skeleton under the ground. If he was lucky enough to have been chosen to go and live with Jesus, I felt we should have been pleased, for his sake, even though we missed him.

(F. 47)

As a small child I had no idea of it at all and at the age of 5 or 6 said quite cheerfully to my father when we were passing the churchyard, "You'll soon be in there, Daddy, won't you?" I was very fond of my grandfather, a retired headmaster, who lived with us and, though going blind, taught us to read. He was quite blind for the last few years of his life. To me he was a wonderful example of patience and gentleness, and he taught me the importance of obeying the rules. When he was dying, peacefully, at 84, I used to sit with him alone for quite long periods, while the adults had a breather. When he died one night my aunt, to break it gently, said "Grandpa can see now". This seemed to me such a wonderful thing for him that I could think of nothing else. I could not understand the grief of my mother and aunt, or their putting on horrid black satin blouses. I felt cheerful, often saying "Grandpa can SEE", and was even gently upbraided for this and reminded that I had been in floods of tears over the recent death of my cat; but then I saw the cat's lifeless body; also I knew people lived on in some way, but did not know about animals.

(F. 68)

In 1918 my grannie whom I quite liked died at our home, the parents being away on holiday at the time. The maid said to me "Your grannie died in the night. You mustn't go into her room. Your parents will be home tonight". Well I waited till the maid had gone off somewhere and tiptoed in to have a look at grannie. Lifting up the sheet that covered the face I was surprised to see nothing there but a waxwork figure . . . Grannie had very definitely gone and left behind a mask like the cases grubs left behind when they became butterflies. The parents probably thought me very unfeeling when I didn't cry at the funeral. I felt it all to be rather a waste of time, like burying with pomp Grannie's old clothes.

(F. 64)

Death was taken for granted when I was a child. It just happened; we found dead birds and played funerals, or saw dead toads squashed flat on the road . . . I must have been five at the time when my mother felt she should enlighten me about death. She was at her most embarrassing when enlightening us about anything. She was sitting on a garden seat and I running about picking daisies and didn't want to come when she called. Even at that age one could always feel when she was going to be embarrassing. "I want to talk to you darling about Mr. — ", she said. After some time I suddenly tumbled to what she was trying to get over and said, relieved, "Oh you mean he's dead". Shocked, mother said, "Oh darling, you do know about death?" "Of course" (scornfully), "everything dies some time" or words to that effect. How in a clergyman's family she can have imagined that we wouldn't know about death, I can't think. She had probably been reading a book on "what to tell and when" (the child-care booklets of those days were pretty dim).

(F. 64)

I was made aware of death in an overwhelming way when my father died of cancer when I was 3¾ years old. In their well-meant desire to save me from the worst impact of death, grown-ups to my insistent questioning gave me an explanation of the terrible things I knew were happening which they thought would be appropriate for a child of my age to understand. I remember distinctly the frustration and exasperation I felt with adults for what I knew was failing to tell me the whole truth, which the "mature" part of me would be able to take better than what I knew were fairy-tales to shield me. Consequently I felt utterly bewildered and the horrifying unknown aspect of death oppressed me. Only when my mother explained to me her own firm belief, that his spirit continued to be with us and watched over us for our good, helping to guide us, did I accept her explanation, which confirmed my own feelings.

(F. 56)

I think I was always aware of death and never afraid of it. I distinctly remember walking home to lunch from school one day — aged about 8 or 9 — when I passed an old-fashioned funeral hearse with everything draped in black. It struck me forcibly and like lightning that the dead person must be looking on thinking how silly all this was, when he or she was so happy. It was, to me, a very satisfying experience.

(F. 54)

Death as part of a natural cycle

As a small child I seemed to be surrounded by lots of kind great-aunts and uncles who died from time to time. Even now I have clear impressions of them lying in their coffins surrounded by sorrowing relatives. In spite of having loved them and knowing I should miss their company, I felt calmly detached rather than distressed. It was as if I instinctively felt only the wonder and unity of life and that death is merely part of its natural cycle. Thus I never feared death. I can only vaguely recall this calm detached feeling now. When I became adult I absorbed the sophistication of our complex materialistic civilization and sometimes shed bitter tears. But when I re-read a childhood poem (Thomas Hood's *I Remember*) I was affected by the poignancy of his lines describing his childish impression of the tall trees being "close against the sky": "It was a childish ignorance, but now 'tis little joy to know I'm further off from heaven than when I was a boy". This reminded me how far I had travelled from my childhood nearness to some kind of eternal reality.

(F. 44)

Death seemed to me great and wonderful — "eloquent and mighty" would have done well had I known the phrase — but never, in our circle, final.

(F. 59)

At the age of about 7-11 years I would torment myself with the idea of darkness and pain and suffering of a mental nature. Thoughts of total nothing for ever and ever and ever. However deep down inside I always knew, sometimes more strongly than others, that it was just a sensational game that I played with myself, as death seemed the only subject which related to IT in any way. I knew that IT could not die as IT could only go back to where IT came from; which is no death at all. This realisation was accompanied by an affirmative rush of energy.

(F. 28)

I had only a vague idea that one "continued". The idea of "heaven" complete with harps and angels and the literal idea of hell seemed too ridiculous; I had not formulated any other ideas on this. I knew that heaven and hell could not be up and down,

128

and that neither could exist in a physical place. All in all, I knew what was not true about death, but did not know what was true.

(F. 24)

Positive attitudes

My early feelings about human death were that it was something exciting, and desirable, in fact a return to something one understood and knew. I can remember remarking one day that I could remember what it was like before I was born, and the atmosphere of embarrassment and unbelief with which this was received, together with the realisation that though I knew they thought I was lying, in actual fact I did not feel that I was, though truthfully I could not remember much more than light in which there were presences.

(F. 67)

I was afraid of death but at the same time curious because I could not believe that this was the very end. I instinctively felt that death was a new beginning in some way.

(F. 49)

Already at a very young age I started trying to think of death as of a great friend and teacher. I have always believed that one should cultivate a friendly relation to death. My view of death never came out of a negation of life, but on the contrary out of its utmost assertion.

(F. 60)

Death was always surrounded by mystery and wonder; as far back as I can remember I thought this way. My visits to the graveyard made me very happy and peaceful and there was no thought of fear. I remember when my grandfather died the thought before he died of not seeing him again brought me to tears, but just before Mum told us I guessed what had happened and felt peacefully happy about the whole thing. Both his funeral and cremation service were very moving and enriching experiences. I was very satisfied with the whole thing.

(F. 16)

Death as desirable

I can only remember as a young child really longing to die so that I could be with God and Jesus and find out what this wonderful heaven was like. I certainly never thought of it in any other way then and accepted it without question.

(F. 25)

I was, generally speaking, a restless and "naughty" child, but at some point my mother's insistence that one had to be good in order to get to heaven got home, and for ONE WHOLE DAY I managed to be "good". The day ended in a state of sheer bliss. I was in fact ripe for heaven, and on going to bed (every detail is recallable even now and has always been so) I was persuaded that I would die and go to heaven. My picture of heaven was first "gentle Jesus", a conventional picture in blue robe, in a green meadow waiting for me, with other children and golden light in the background. Vaguely aware that my parents, especially my mother, would miss me, I wept a few tears for them and fell slowly and gently fast asleep, so convinced that I was on my way out of this world that next morning's awaking was an almighty shock; for my first sensation was to know I was in bed and that all was as when I had gone to sleep. I was BACK — but coincident with the awakening disappointment was a sense of the Jesus I had expected to meet, for an inner voice said "not for a long time, but one day" and I saw stretching into the distance a sort of path or way, but then I was just a disappointed child and cried.

(F. 60)

10

MORALITY AND SIGNIFICANCE

Let me return to Edwin Muir:

> My brothers and sisters were new creatures like myself, not in
> time (for time still sat on the wrist of each day with its
> wings folded), but in a vast, boundless calm. I could not have put
> all this into words then, but this is what I felt and what we all
> feel before we become conscious that time moves and that all
> things change . . . We think and feel immortally in our first few
> years, simply because time does not exist for us. We pay no
> attention to time until he tugs us by the sleeve or claps his
> policeman's hand on our shoulder; it is in our nature to ignore
> him, but he will not be ignored.[1]

One of the problems when we come to look at the sense of right
and wrong in childhood is that we tend to judge it in terms of our
own notions of morality; and this morality is essentially *time-
bound*. A moral act, that is, involves an element of calculation;
we judge a man by, among other things, the thought he gives to
the consequences of his actions. To be well meaning is not
enough; he must also be responsible, ready to answer at some
future date for what he does now. Time may in fact clap his
policeman's hand on a child's shoulder earlier than we generally
imagine. It seems certain that children are capable of
deliberation and a sense of responsibility long before they can
find words to formulate these feelings and capacities. But more
important than this, is there native to childhood some *timeless*
imperative, independent of the categories of thought and
calculation? An imperative, it may be, later adopted by reason

as the sanction for its ethical structures but prior to them both in time and logic? "In my childhood we daren't let our elders know how mature we were. As for religious feelings and ideas, they'd been there all along". Can the same be said for moral feelings?

Asked whether the formation of their sense of right and wrong was entirely due to their upbringing, or whether there was ever a sense of conflict between such a socially-induced conscience and any religious feelings of their own, almost exactly half our correspondents gave a "yes" to the first question while implying or stating a "no" to the second (see Appendix, p. 165). Here again, the subject demands a deeper and more subtle study than the replies to such questions allow. For example, absence of conflict may indicate harmony; it may equally indicate a total lack of contact. Religion and morality may have chimed happily together, or they may have been felt to have nothing to do with one another. As an investigation into the origins of moral feeling this is clearly quite inadequate.

Where these replies do help is in showing how childhood does not simply conceive of the world as it is, but also as it has to be. Reality just is the way it is; to act as though it were not, or to suit your own convenience, is — well, wrong is far too weak a word, being associated with prohibitions and transgressions that only derive their meaning from the recognition of a greater reality. "Goodness", writes one correspondent, "was an intuitive sense of recognition of truth, something you for ever after look for in tone, in action, in silence, in expression, in art, in nature." The ethical sense of shame was also real, no less important, but different, coming from consideration for others, awareness of moral cowardice, shabby evasions, self-deceit. "The deeper sense of humility comes from religious experience: that sense of recognition of truth." What the adult in fact thinks of as a particular moral sense, an ability to think of things in terms of right and wrong, is only a polarization of what in childhood is a more diffused, all-inclusive feeling. When we learn to use a map the first thing is to get it the right way up, with the North at the top. Then we can plot our position by reference to latitude and longitude; we can know where we are in relation to other known points. It is in this spirit that an adult will talk about "applying moral standards". Like a map-reference, they enable him to "know where he stands". Without them we may feel lost. But we may also have lost something. "I wanted to be good but from an early stage I felt that goodness ought to have something to do with joy. I felt negative goodness to be wrong." "My early sense of right and wrong was vague until taught; a much earlier sense of kind and unkind was very intense and goes back to my first memories of one or one and a half years." "I always felt that 'whole-heartedness' was the only right and that to do something because it was right but without really wanting to was wrong." Here I recall a telling phrase from the psychotherapist Peter Lomas, who speaks of a "passionate commitment to spontaneous living".[2] This he says is what so many adults have lost in their obsessional concern for emotional detachment as the key to mature development. It is surely the reality of these raw feelings that gives substance to a morality that is built round them, and gives the lie to one that does not do them justice. "I would not be forced to do anything that was against my inner feelings . . . It was impossible to be true to yourself if you obeyed laws blindly". Another writes: "At a more basic level I feel that one's ethical code is based on what one really is." This brings us back to the search for authenticity: the feeling that nothing can ever outweigh the authority of what has come home to us in the most personal way. The shallow proprieties of social life may exact a superficial assent but experiences of this kind, "felt in the blood and felt along the heart", persist at a deeper level.

The childhood vision, which gave such an embracing sense of evolving life, light and meaning in the universe, was the fundamental measure against which I tested everything else. I saw people and things in terms of quality and quantity of light: the presence of light, or its lack, was my only yardstick of right and wrong. One outstanding and repeated experience was that, when I tried to speak to adults of the light, or tried to live by its implicit truth, this was often met with blank astonishment or, as I grew older, active annoyance. I was continually told not to be insolent when speaking what I thought was the straight truth as I saw it, however wrongly. And I learned only slowly to compromise with the accepted norms and to keep silence on things that really mattered to me. Gradually I built a laughing and shallow persona to hide behind, which made me more socially accepted.

(F. 43)

This however cannot be the last word. To represent the child's view of the world as always dominated by this thorough-going intuitionism would not be true to the general trend of replies to these questions. After all, here we have over three hundred people all of whom have recorded some spontaneous experience of a religious kind from childhood; yet half of them felt no conflict between their religious feelings and the ethical standards of their upbringing, and in the other half reactions ranged from outright rejection to a mild ambivalence: their ideas of right and wrong might have had an internal source but the acceptance of conventional teaching gave them little trouble. It is easy to set up false oppositions here: to contrast conventional values with personal experience and then see every decision as a synthesis reached through a reconciliation of thesis and antithesis. We may think of a convention as a sort of package deal, compounded of expediency and compromise and artificially foisted on a new generation which naturally rejects it in favour of its own experience. But like traditions, all conventions have their roots in experience. Furthermore, nothing could be more unnatural than to be born into a society without conventions; it would hardly be a society at all. Hence the great difficulty many of our correspondents have in distinguishing which of their ideas or feelings were spontaneous or taught: "No doubt my parents formed the basis of my moral sense, but I feel that much of it was quite instinctive and might well have developed on its own": "I never remember feeling coerced; the teaching became my own convictions". And where there is no teaching, a vacuum may be felt, a deep need for "the truth and security of moral standards".

Authority in fact no less than authenticity is a natural element in a healthy and mature moral sense. The two words, so superficially similar, have very different roots: in the search for authenticity the initiative is with the self, while authority is accepted from outside. It is by the internalizing of authority that an authentic morality develops. This is the key to the old debate about the relation of religious to moral education.

Can moral feelings, or even moral habits, be instilled or acquired in isolation from religious beliefs? The quick answer is "yes, of course", especially if by "religious" we think of the traditional forms. Anyway, the vast majority of all our moral decisions are not made with one eye on eternity, but by a simple reckoning of practical consequences, a purely utilitarian calculus. And yet ultimately this will not do. There may be less of the sense of unreality in our new moral education programmes than in some other sectors of the curriculum; but they are not immune. As one correspondent puts it, "The emotion of significance seems to me to exist independently of any moral code". It will not ultimately be ignored. We may get encouraging results in programmes of moral education, progress which can be measured by the success of community service and social responsibility projects. The considerate way of life may be built into the curriculum. And yet, and yet . . . What happens to this so reasonably-based morality in an emergency? The giant Antaeus was all-powerful so long as he kept contact with his mother Earth. Once lifted off the ground, his strength was gone and he was strangled with ease. Who then to-day are the true down-to-earth realists? Those who give priority to practical programmes of social action? Or those who know that moral convictions, however time-bound the world in which they must operate, must also be rooted in some awareness of the timeless if they are to survive crisis? Of course we need both. But which of the two are we to-day most in danger of forgetting? No-one denies the need for a thorough examination of the values on which our society should be based, and for the development of a curriculum that will reinforce them. Never was the individual under greater pressure to conform to demands of every kind — who ever called this a permissive society?

How with this rage shall beauty hold a plea
Whose action is no stronger than a flower?

In the face of all these stresses it is easy to lose nerve and to forget the sheer power of what is there to be appealed to, which is not the baseless fabric of a vision but "the living tissue of life itself . . . both fragile yet immensely strong, and utterly good and beneficent".

135

No-one, then, would wish to set up the inner oracle as the sole sanction for morality, or wholeheartedness as the only right without qualification. But if our ethic is to be more than a system of prohibitions it must be based on a capacity to respond positively to all experience. There is a Rabbinic saying: "A man will have to give account in the judgement day of every good thing which he might have enjoyed and did not."[3] The idea is one that is not easily expressed in English. This was brought home to me when I had to translate a letter from a correspondent in Vienna:

> Quite late in life I came to realise that my most significant religious experience had come when as a small child I was walking along my usual road in a built-up area in my home town and, looking up, saw with inexpressible joy and thankfulness that the sky was blue. The power of this basic experience persisted even at a time when, some twenty years later, I had come to feel that my personal life was without happiness or meaning. I was aware that not all acorns could germinate and grow up into oaks, and that the beauty and greatness of the whole is not in any way diminished thereby; I knew that many individual things, many individual people, do not necessarily come to fulfilment. But when in course of time my thinking became more mature I realised that the emotional attitude of *Seinsbejahung* was a moral act, that it was the very foundation of all morality, of all *Weltanschauung*.
>
> It is joy in fact that is the basis of all life. Joy, that is, leads, by reflection on consciousness, to *Ichbejahung* and this in turn matures into *Seinsbejahung*, an attitude that underlies all the value judgements that are really significant in our lives.

(F. 63)

We have long ago given up trying to translate *"Weltan-schauung*; we might equally well adopt *Seinsbejahung* into our language, as we have no tolerable equivalent. There is something alien to the whole Protestant tradition in this attitude of saying "yes" to life, to existence, to reality. The acceptance of *Ichbejahung*, saying "yes" to one's self, is equally hard to combine with the sense of sin so assiduously cultivated in some branches of Christianity. Yet unless we recognize the force of these impulses (which is not the same as letting them take over) and see them as a natural and instinctive element in human nature, no morality that is set up in competition with them will have a chance. The same is true of religion. "If we ask 'what is the meaning of life?' ", writes Margaret Isherwood, "our question is too large. We should begin by becoming aware of the questions life puts to us."[4] But if our answers to these questions are always to start with a negative, we shall miss the point of much experience that might have been religious.

*   *   *

Further Examples

Parental teaching as formative

I think the formation of my sense of right and wrong was entirely due to the teaching of my parents, especially my mother whom I adored, and her slightest disapproval of any misbehaviour or wrongdoing on my part broke my heart.

(F. 54)

My mother's morality was very rigid and from her I acquired a strong sense of right and wrong, which led to an equally strong sense of guilt if any of the rules were infringed. Love, in the Christian sense, did not enter into it. My parents, so far as I am aware, were the only people to give me a set of values, emphasis being placed on success by my father, and on cleanliness and righteousness by my mother. I think I must have been a terrible prig, and don't remember questioning these values until very much later in life.

(F. 45)

Parental teaching as supportive

Certainly the influence of my parents exemplifying the working of right and wrong in daily life was always present. But I sometimes think that my own feelings would automatically have led me in the same way. Possibly without the help of my parents' example my confidence in such feelings might have wilted. I do not feel that what I think now is essentially my parents' teaching. It is essentially something which has grown in me.

(M. 62)

Just as I was taught physical laws, e.g. if I put my hand in the fire it would hurt, so the spiritual laws of God were real too, e.g. whatsoever a man soweth that shall he also reap. I suppose this may seem a socially induced conscience, but I never remember feeling coerced; the teaching became my own convictions, and to this day they are still constant.

(F. 56)

Compassion

My sense of right and wrong was I think solely given to me by my parents and those around me, though this never troubled me unduly. I remember stealing quite often, knowing it to be wrong, but I don't think I ever worried about it. What I wanted I took — until about the age of 11, as I was about to take some particularly nice marbles, I had a flash of insight into what the girl would feel like when she found them missing. The thought of her distress cured me of stealing, not the knowledge that what I was doing was wrong.

(F. 30)

Fundamentally I think the sense of right and wrong, despite the fact that I was given a rule-of-thumb measure by my parents, derived from my own psychological make-up; e.g. I recall that I used to ask my mother for coins to give to a hunchbacked dwarf who sold bootlaces and pencils in central Glasgow. As a child, the sight of this unfortunate twisted my gut with compassion. I have a little doubt that my compassion (emotion, plus a sense that it would be wrong to ignore him) sprang from my own childish sense of inadequacy. I experienced no conflict between socially-induced conscience and subjective conscience. (M. 44)

There was conflict, yes. Socially induced conscience was to do with dressing tidily and going to church, and singing well, and looking good in front of the parishioners, and not letting the side down. This seemed quite different from loving God and loving my neighbour. The genuine compassion that my father showed for the sick and upset among his patients was completely different from the relationships within the parish, somehow. The compassion seemed so much more real, and so much more religious to me, and yet it was not part of any religious teaching as it was given to me then.

(F. 39)

The Authority of Feeling

Social conscience was quite different from religious feelings. When I started to read poetry, hear music, see pictures, I recognized something contained in a form that I had been aware of in a formless way; urgency, rawness of feeling, a balance between the nice and the not-nice, authenticity, wildness.

(F. 49)

I had my own code of behaviour at an early age. This involved being true to myself. I would not be forced to do anything that was against my inner feelings. At home this was understood, so there was little cause for conflict. I would try to explain about a questionable act so that my brothers would not be blamed. I could not understand punishment. To me, it was a fault in the elders if they did not understand how the mistake had been made. There was no punishment except my father's hurt, but I suddenly realised there was justice in punishment. To obey a law merely because it was a law has always troubled me. It was impossible to be true to yourself if you obeyed laws blindly. I don't know why I always acted on my own judgement. My parents did not deliberately make us aware of right and wrong. Only when I did something foolish was I reprimanded, never beaten. I think that having so few definite rules to obey, I was thrown back on my own judgement, found truth either by trial and error, or by obedience to the truth in me. I may have been influenced in my surface behaviour patterns by my parents. I may have accepted their moral code. But hidden within, the evolving, true self was unaffected except by my own creative thought. The reality in all

139

of us, the soul which is the seed of the spirit, has its own path to follow unaffected by anyone or anything. That which is outside us is a shadow.

(F. 65)

Superficially, yes. My parents affected me at the level of social codes, and by encouraging certain types of value and behaviour patterns, so that I no doubt felt good when conforming to them. At a more basic level, I feel that one's ethical code is based on what one really is. I adapted to the code in a group in which I found myself as easily as the chameleon adapts his colour; enormous conflict ensued if this code was at variance with my real nature, and I would soon drift off, as I do now, in order to be myself.

(F. 41)

Conflicts

I am not sure whether I have a sense of right and wrong. I am suppose I must have. If I do anything I think is wrong, I am sorry and try to make amends. Having done this and resolved not to do it again, I can eliminate all feelings of guilt. In fact from schooldays onwards, I loathed the sense of guilt and sin induced by Christianity, also the injustice of God in the Bible stories, and the wallowing in blood and crucifixion and sacrifice, and the cannibalistic Mass and Communion.

(F. 65)

I can remember an instance of conflict between socially induced conscience and following the commands of Christ when I was about nine years old. I and two other children, having nothing better to do, and being sent out for a boring walk together, fell into a discussion of a horrible-looking old woman who passed with a bundle on her back. We decided that Jesus Christ's teaching was that we should go after her and carry her bundle for her. The charm of this existed solely in the fact that to do such a thing (the old woman was filthily dirty) was in direct opposition to the known rules of our nurses and elders — but how much less important were they than God. We were after her like a flash. The result was not what we had hoped: three merry children all eager to carry her bundle did not inspire trust in the old woman, and we

140

departed scared at the sound of her uncomprehended cursing. It was not the only time we found that the actual following of New Testament advice did not seem to work out.

(F. 65)

The formation of my sense of right and wrong may have been influenced by the saying of prayers at night, but I think it unlikely. I think it more likely that it was a gradual development of my own, innate or otherwise, thought processes. For instance, on two occasions I went out with a gang. On the first occasion they stole apples and plums, and although I did not join them (not through fear — I was rarely afraid) they invited me to eat them. I told them I would not because one of the Commandments stated "Thou shalt not steal". On the other occasion they went round to Woolworths for similar reasons. Again I refused, and needless to say I was not again included in the activities of the gang. I remember feeling very angry and it landed me in a fight with a boy much bigger than myself when I objected to him swearing on a Sunday. I was never afraid to fight, because I felt that if I chose the right then I could not lose. Looking back, these things seem irrational and quite unreasonable, but at that time I defended what I felt to be right in the only way I knew, and street fights on council house estates were common. This happened when I was at primary and junior school; when I went to secondary school I had grown out of this phase and despised seeing others fight. What I felt was more like indignation than conflict because a socially induced conscience has always been very secondary to any religious feeling that I had or still have.

(F. 37)

In the nursery we had to say "I'm sorry", but I had the impression that it was a formula for settling scores and restoring peace, rather than that my state of mind should correspond with the words I spoke. The supernatural was out: so was formal doctrine in any shape or form. People who subscribed to a dogma were assumed not to have thought the matter out properly. I seem to recall feeling slightly puzzled that my mother and Darwin were the only ones to be right; but it was good to feel one would be loyal to a martyr for the truth. To agree with the crowd would have been comfortable, but I was never tempted, being a Protestant by temperament. Somewhere deep down in me I

141

began, perhaps about eleven, to sense the absurdity of supposing that the teaching of Christ had been distorted by the church for nearly two thousand years, only to be correctly interpreted by the rationalists of my mother's youth.

(F. 50)

The conflict was the other way round. I wanted passionately the security of moral teaching, and particularly of spiritual teaching, that was not forthcoming in my home or school. I tried unsuccessfully to bring the teaching of my grandparents into my home life; a disaster, as that teaching was taken personally as a judgement on my parents, and no-one else had the slightest desire for the truth and security of moral standards that I tried to hard to inflict on them.

(F. 55)

The voice of God

I do not like the phrase "socially-induced conscience". Children are much more honest than most adults know. God does teach people quite independently.

(F. 60)

I should say I had a sense of right and wrong not determined by anyone else; I feel sure of this. But I don't know that it was ever in conflict with my socially-induced conscience. It was different from rather than in conflict with. Also, when different, I had no hesitation in trusting in my innate sense: I trusted it above everything. But how far it was really determined by outside influences I do not know. I felt it was determined by God. When I heard the opinion that conscience is the voice of God I knew this was right.

(F. 64)

The sense of rightness

At some level of "emotion" I am so reassured of the ultimate goodness inherent in everything that all the evidence to the contrary in the world around me seems suddenly to be of no importance relatively; and the strength derived from this feeling, though the experience itself may be put aside or even denied by reason — nevertheless is strong enough to be the basis of an optimism in living. I remember having this sense of a "rightness" in the universe when I was about six years old.

(F. 49)

At the age of seven I was lastingly aware of the superhuman force of righteousness. Religious background and training was slight, and this awareness was sparked off by something that might appear quite trivial. Standing at home in the garden with another child I mentioned to her the name of a flower that had been given to us both a few days earlier. Immediately and to my astonishment this naming was contradicted. It seemed terribly important to me that rightness should be upheld, and I appealed to a nearby grown-up for support. Alas, this was seen as a personal issue and was brusquely put aside. I felt very much alone in a world which I believed couldn't make sense if such untruths were not only allowed but deemed to be unimportant. I can vividly recall how I stood reaching outward and upward (in my mind) for comfort. Comfort did come, not from any fatherly figure, but from a strong assurance that there was a governing power of universal righteousness. This experience I kept to myself.

(F. 47)

11

SOMETHING MORE

"Experience that might have been religious": I have at various points indicated how unsatisfactory some traditional criteria are. The religious is not to be identified with the mystical; it does not have its roots in morality, but rather the other way round; it is not to be defined in relation to religion. But if my approach has seemed to be negative, what I have rejected have been the limitations that others would set to a concept as wide as life itself, in fact wider. It is the function of definitions, in so far as they are precise, to limit, to exclude. To start with a definition of what might constitute religious experience would have been as mistaken as to hope to have reached one by the end. Faced with a similar problem E. R. Goodenough observes: "Only as we describe the various conflicting elements associated with such words can we finally arrive at a meaning that includes their complexities."[1] I hope I have done enough to show that the original vision of childhood may be simple in its immediate unity but as uniquely complex as a fingerprint if we attempt to analyse it into its elements. Goodenough continues: "In important matters we understand not as we simplify but as we can tolerate the paradoxical."

Some may still feel it intolerably paradoxical to base a study of childhood on the records of those who have in years at least left it so long behind. Yet perhaps, as in Brooke's sentimental poem,

The years that take the best away

144

Give something in the end.

It may be that it is only among the dead leaves of a lifetime's experience, that time-rich humus in which we may see nothing but decomposition and decay, that childhood can grow to maturity — its own maturity. I was talking not long ago to Donald Nicholl who had spent some time as visiting professor in an American university. At the beginning of one academic year a group of students who had just returned from a year in Europe under the university's Study Abroad programme were invited to dinner by the chancellor, and each was asked to recount his "experience of Europe" and make an assessment of it. After they had all spoken, Professor Nicholl was asked to comment on their experiences. "I began", he said, "by saying that I found some difficulty in doing this because they had not yet had their experience of Europe; and that maybe in another fifty years they would have had it sufficiently for me to be able to make some worthwhile comment." One might say then, in justification of such a study as this, that to have attempted an assessment of the childhood experience of any of these writers at an earlier age would have been in some respects at least premature; that they would not yet have had their experience, or not yet had it sufficiently for a proper judgement to be made of it. A remarkable instance of this slow process comes from a man who had never been able to forget a vaguely mystical experience he had had more than fifty years before. At the time, and for long after, it had little effect on him: "I was the same man after as before". Reflecting on its subsequent influence he is only sure of one thing: it had not had the effect it might have if he had made more of it. He goes on:

> The remarkable thing, as I now see, about such seeds, stored as bare memories of experiences which in the past have fallen on unreceptive ground, is their capacity to remain dormant for long periods, perhaps waiting inertly for an auspicious change in the soil which contains them.

Later in his letter the writer actually thanks us for having brought him to reflect on this long-buried experience, and so having enabled it to germinate.

At what stage if any that experience is to be called religious cannot of course be determined without further study both of the original event and what it subsequently came to mean for him. But we can see in it one element necessary to any experience that is to be so regarded: the response that leads to growth. It is not enough for the experience to occur; one must say "yes" to it. "The most frequent religious sensations I have experienced", writes another correspondent, "I can best describe as acknowledgements." Where there is no sensitivity to "the questions life puts to us" that essential element of growth can hardly begin.[2]

Some people will not like this kind of languge. To write of Life with a capital L is to them mere sentimental rhetoric, a sign of mental laziness. In fact, to say that we must not ask for the meaning of life but rather pay attention to the questions life puts to us is a neat expression of a profound truth. It does not excuse us from metaphysical effort; it tells us that metaphysics must start from personal experience. The theoretical discussion of ultimate questions may be acceptable in an academic milieu; but to face them at the point where for you or me they arise, in the form in which they arise — this is what ultimately matters; only then can we know these questions to be, in fact, ultimate — a point which theology, which generally begins where experience leaves off, might more often consider.

Of course to speak of "Life" in this way need not be the limit of our philosophical ambitions. It can sometimes be equivalent to no more than a resigned shrug of the shoulders: "c'est la vie". To stop here is indeed intellectual laziness. "Life" in this sense is more than mere biological survival: it is more than any particular life, yours or mine or anybody else's. It is "la condition humaine", it is "Sein", it is the totality of human experience — and then more, because what gives form to life must be found not only in it but beyond it, as in sculpture the material is given form and significance by the contour and surface that are its limits. And here we reach the notion of the transcendent.

"Religious experience", writes one correspondent, "is any experience that causes me to feel that there is a 'something-more-than' situation." Stripped of its mystique, the transcendent is no more than the sense of this "something more". Meaning, after all, is to be found not in the meaningful object or situation itself but always beyond it. This is the point of Georges Braque's profound remark that when art abandons nature it becomes mere decoration. To be significant art no less than life must point beyond itself: art for art's sake is as meaningless as life for life's sake. This then is the second element necessary to the concept of the religious: there must be a response not merely to life but to all those moments and encounters that give it meaning. "Three moments of such realization I can remember quite clearly: one was at a football match, seeing two seagulls fly across a snow-covered pitch, one at a ship-launching, and one on a dockside, having turned around in the dusk to see suddenly a fire in a warehouse about a mile down the river. Each of these experiences was for some reason deeply religious." The last thing I want to do is to trivialize the transcendent or strip it of its mystery. But where does one start? With the Doctrine of the Trinity? The Sistine Chapel? The Divine Comedy? To take as examples such supreme expressions of intellectual or artistic aspiration too easily suggests that personal experience of the transcendent is something that you or I can rarely hope for, or something which at best we can only have through the creative insights of the mystic, the genius or the saint. Religious experience may open up to us what Plato conceived of as the world of being, but it must also have its roots in the world of becoming. Many people to-day find themselves more deeply moved, in a way they will describe as in some sense religious, by Van Gogh's old boots than by the sublime vision of Michelangelo. And this significance of the insignificant is a theme central to the biblical, the Christian tradition. The still small voice, the grain of mustard seed, the one coin lost, the single sparrow dead — these are the stuff of which religious experience is made. True, as Browning said, "a man's reach should exceed his grasp", and there is no knowing where such experience will end. But the study of it must also include the often humdrum or even apparently degrading circumstances in which it may start, and those at first sight quite unremarkable moments that touch off that recurrent urge in us all to make some sense of the world. Recurrent? In us all? More usually

147

intermittent or spasmodic, in some perhaps seemingly atrophied; but still surely recognizable when it comes.

> After the experience of the sense of presence I knew, as Walt Whitman expressed it, that there was more to me than was found between my hat and my shoes. It was up to me to find out more about that MORE; and so, as I see it, my minuscule will was linked up with the will that our forefathers called God. I don't know what that power is, nor do I call it God. But by it I live and in my slow, often frustrated effort to learn means of communication with it I grow, inch by inch, into a person more nearly resembling a human being than was ever imagined by me to be possible. This power beyond my own ego is not altogether beyond it or separate from it. It is as personal and "of me" as the colour of my eyes, is friendly and reliable, resourceful and companionable. But on the far side of "me" it is a mystery with respect to which I put my hand on my mouth.
>
> (F. 73)

The great majority of those whose experience led me to make this study are men and women in whom the original vision of childhood has never wholly faded. But are they typical? And what of the rest of us who have no such memories? If the child within me dies a little more each day, how, asks Marcel, am I to be faithful to myself? And when I cannot do this, "I am no longer there, I do not exist any more". In Brancusi's words, when we cease to be children, we are already dead. But if childhood in the wider, timeless sense is in some mysterious fashion connected, or even to be identified with, that kind of awareness that is truly to be called religious, it could be that by learning once more to respond to the demands made upon us by the something-more-than situation we may discover that there is still a spark of life in the child within each one of us.

148

NOTES

Chapter 1

1. Liam Hudson, *Contrary Imaginations* (Pelican Books, London, 1967), p. 17.

2. I am not referring here to "the Child" of Transactional Analysis. There is a great deal to be learnt from the recognition that in each of us there is a Parent, an Adult and a Child at work. Dr. Thomas Harris *(I'm O.K. — You're O.K.,* Pan Books, London, 1973) has made a most useful contribution to self-analysis for which I for one am grateful. Anything that will help us to come to terms with the infantile as well as the authoritarian elements in ourselves is to be welcomed. But in the concept of childhood I include rather more than he does. It is interesting incidentally to note a certain ambivalence in Harris' own description of 'the Child', which includes both "the Natural Child" and "the Adaptive Child" (op. cit., p. 121); also that his view of religious experience is one in which "the Child" has an important part to play (op. cit., pp. 226f.).

3. Constantin Brancusi, quoted in David Lewis, *Constantin Brancusi* (Academy Editions, London, 1974), p. 20.

4. J. Piaget & B. Inhelder, *The Psychology of the Child,* tr. Helen Weaver (Routledge & Kegan Paul, 1969), p. 128.

5. J. Piaget, *The Child's Conception of the World,* tr. J. & A. Tomlinson, (Routledge & Kegan Paul, 1929), p. 62.

6. J. Piaget, op. cit., p. 86.

7. Consider for example, a recent statement from Mr. John Rae, Headmaster of Westminster School and currently chairman of the Headmasters' Conference: "For too long the teachers and education theorists have claimed the right to tell the nation what the children shall learn. It is time for the nation, which

provides the money and suffers the consequences, to assert its will." Reported in The Times, 3rd February, 1977.

8. The dangers of a premature adjustment to "adult reality" are emphasized by Alexander Lowen in his book *The Language of the Body* (Collier Macmillan, London, 1971). He deplores the tendency to have young children mature too rapidly, and points out that the development of "a good reality function" depends to a large extent on "a full and pleasurable childhood".

9. R. Goldman, *Religious Thinking from Childhood to Adolescence* (Routledge & Kegan Paul, 1964), p. 226.

10. Consider for example his final judgement on St. Teresa of Avila "So paltry were these" (her religious ideals) "that I confess my only feeling in reading her has been pity that so much vitality of soul should have found such poor employment . . . There is absolutely no human use in her, or sign of any general human interest." *The Varieties of Religious Experience* (Longmans, Green, London, 1903), pp. 346ff.

11. William James, op. cit., p. 486.

12. William James, op. cit., p. 45.

13. Aristotle, *Physics,* 199B.

Chapter 2

1. Edwin Muir, *Autobiography* (Faber, 1938), p. 33.

2. Plato, *Phaedrus,* 266 B.

3. Henri Poincaré, *Mathematical Creation*, tr. G. B. Halsted, in Brewster Ghiselin (ed.), *The Creative Process* (Mentor Books, 1952), p. 40.

4. David Elkind, *The Origins of Religion in the Child*, in Review of Religious Research, Vol. 12, No. 1, pp. 35-42 (Fall, 1970).

5. William James, *The Varieties of Religious Experience* (Longmans Green, London) pp. 378f.

6.   William James, op. cit., pp. 380f.

7.   Ben-Ami Scharfstein, *Mystical Experience* (Blackwell, 1973), p. 169.

Chapter 3

1.   W. Wordsworth, *Tintern Abbey.*

2.   W. Wordsworth, *The Prelude* (1850), 8: 53ff.

3.   As e.g. in *Mysticism Sacred and Profane* (O.U.P., 1957).

Chapter 4

1.   Gabriel Marcel, *Homo Viator,* tr. Emma Craufurd (Gollancz, 1951), p. 131.

2.   S. Freud, *Works, Standard Edition*, (Hogarth Press, 1959), Vol. 21, p. 177. Quoted in Anthony Storr, *The Dynamics of Creation* (Pelican Books, 1976), p. 18. I am much indebted to Dr. Storr for the lucid account given in this book of Freud's views on art and its supposed origins in infantile frustration.

3.   E. Erikson, *Childhood and Society* (Penguin Books, 1965), p. 32.

4.   André Malraux, *Antimemoirs,* tr. Kilmartin (Penguin, 1970), p. 10.

5.   "It is not enough to understand *about* children, one has to come to understand *them.* Such a kind of understanding is based primarily on an understanding of one's self. No matter how much this understanding requires to be augmented by all sorts of relevant study, its primary source lies in the understanding one has, and can gain, of one's own 'childhood', that is of the child still active within oneself". Ben Morris in J. W. Tibble (ed.) *The Study of Education* (Routledge and Kegan Paul, 1965), pp. 169f.

6.   Compare Jung's insistence that of the four functions of the psyche *feeling* should rank with *thinking* as rational, in contrast

to the other two, *sensation* and *intuition.* "Feeling is a kind of judging, differing however, from an intellectual judgement in that it does not aim at establishing an intellectual conviction but is solely concerned with the setting up of a subjective criterion of acceptance or rejection. Feeling like thinking is a rational function since, as is shown by experience, values in general are bestowed according to the laws of reason, just as concepts in general are framed after the laws of reason". C. G. Jung, *Psychological Types,* (London, 1923), pp. 543f.

Chapter 5

1. Quoted by Lionel Trilling, *Sincerity and Authenticity* (O.U.P., 1972), p. 93.

2. John Bowker: "The basic defect of Freud's theory of religion is not that it cannot possibly be right, but that it cannot possibly be wrong: all evidence that superficially appears to contradict the theory is converted to become evidence *for* the theory, because it can be regarded as evidence of repression or of defence against the true nature of what is going on." *The Sense of God* (O.U.P., 1973), pp. 121f.

Chapter 6

1. See his *Inglorious Wordsworths* (Hodder & Stoughton, 1973), throughout but in particular Chapter 8.

2. Peter L. Berger, *A Rumour of Angels* (Pelican Books, London, 1971), p. 84.

3. Quoted by Derek Bok, President of Harvard, in *Harvard Divinity Bulletin,* May 1976, Vol. VI, No. 8, p. 1. Something similar is reflected in the results of a Gallup Poll commissioned for the BBC and reported in The Times of 4th January, 1977. Among other things it indicated that "94% of those questioned regard Britain's economic difficulties as serious but that 74% have little or no confidence in the ability of politicians of any party to put things right".

4. The late Gilbert Ryle, then Professor of Metaphysics at Oxford, was once asked if he did not feel that something had been lost since the more idealistic days of Green and Bosanquet, when it was assumed that philosophy had something of value to say about the meaning and conduct of life. "You mean", replied Ryle, "you miss the booming note?"

5. R. Goldman, op. cit., p. 3.

6. On the other hand much of Zeffirelli's recent film *Jesus of Nazareth* is pure Hofmann.

Chapter 7

1. "Sapienti nihil improvisum accidere potest, nihil omnino novum." Cicero, Tusc. 4, 15, 37.

2. Michael Argyle, *Religious Behaviour* (Routledge & Kegan Paul, 1958), p. 78.

3. See A. M. Greeley, *The Sociology of the Paranormal* (Sage Publications, Chicago, 1975). The same tendency is reported in pilot studies conducted by the Religious Experience Research Unit in Nottingham, U.K.

Chapter 8

1. Lionel Trilling, op. cit., p. 93.

2. M. Buber, *Tales of the Hasidim,* tr. Olga Marx (Thames & Hudson, 1956), Vol. 1., p. 251.

3. M. Buber, *I and Thou,* tr. Gregor Smith (Clark, 1937), p. 57.

4. Otto Rank, *Beyond Psychology* (Dover Publications Inc., New York, 1941), p. 31.

5. Otto Rank, op. cit., p. 16.

Chapter 9

1. Silvia Anthony, *The Discovery of Death in Childhood and Afterwards* (Penguin, 1973), p. 70.

2. Silvia Anthony, op. cit., pp. 162f.

Chapter 10

1. Edwin Muir, op. cit., p. 25.

2. Peter Lomas, *True and False Experience* (Allen Lane, 1973), p. 33. He is commenting on Piaget's insistence that "the essence of the operations of the intelligence is the achievement of knowledge which is independent of the ego". Lomas observers: "The impersonal approach is, in his (Piaget's) view, more correct, more mature than the personal: it is also more detached, being once removed from the original experience. This is an adult-centric view which idealizes a stereotype of mature functioning: calm, omniscient, unemotional detachment in contrast to the frantic and impulsive desires of the child; and the kind of adult it depicts has an obsessional character (albeit one that is acceptable as normal in our society): he has sacrificed his passionate commitment to spontaneous living."

3. Jerusalem Talmud, tractate Kiddushin 4 : 12.

4. Margaret Isherwood, *Searching For Meaning* (Allen & Unwin, 1970) p. 31.

Chapter 11

1. Erwin Ramsdell Goodenough, *The Psychology of Religious Experiences* (Basic Books, New York, 1965), p. 1.

2. It has been suggested to me that this view of religious experience, for which I in any case claim no originality, is similar to that taken by Ian Ramsey, e.g. in his book *Religious Language* (SCM, 1957), more particularly in Chapter 1, entitled "What Kind of Situations

are Religious?". This is certainly a most stimulating book, and I owe a lot to it. The elements of "discernment" and "commitment" which he finds essential in any situation to be called "religious" will be recognized in many of the examples I have quoted in the preceding pages. All the same there are some aspects of his treatment that I find less than satisfactory.

Note first, though, that Ramsey does not speak of "religious experience". (His commentator, Professor Gill, does him no service in taking this section of Ramsey's book as showing "the pattern of religious experience according to Ramsey's interpretation": J. H. Gill, *Ian Ramsey* (Allen & Unwin, 1976), p. 61.) Ramsey's view of a "religious situation" or a "religious man" is essentially retrospective; it is seen from the point of view of one who already has achieved a religious way of life. So he can speak of religious commitment as "a *total* commitment to the *whole* universe" (p. 37) — the italics are his. To Ramsey the religious man is one who has found the meaning of life, not one who is still tentatively feeling around. Furthermore Ramsey sees the "discernment" that is so characteristic of a religious situation as leading naturally, apparently even inevitably, to the "commitment": he speaks of "the 'discernment' from which the commitment follows as a response" (p. 37), "that odd discernment with which religious commitment . . . will necessarily be connected" (p. 47). But as I have I hope shown, in religious experience there may be a very long gap between the discernment and the response, if indeed the latter ever occurs at all. Ramsey however is distinctly unsympathetic to those who find difficulty in making the connection. "To have the discernment without an appropriate commitment is the worst of all religious vices. It is insincerity and hypocrisy" (p. 18). But who is to say what commitment is "appropriate"? There is a faintly authoritarian air here, which also comes out in his conclusion that "for the religious man 'God' is a key word, an irreducible posit, an ultimate of explanation" (p. 47).

This is a perfectly reasonable and consistent view of "what kinds of situation are religious", but it is not mine; nor should it in my judgement be applied without considerable qualifications to the rather different question of what kinds of *experience* are religious.

APPENDIX

THE QUESTIONNAIRE

1. How much do you think that you owe your early religious ideas or feelings to the influence of your family, or to any other individuals who were helpful, whether as models to be imitated or just as sympathetic people to talk to?

2. How far do you feel that your early idea of God was derived from what you saw in your parents?

3. How far do you feel that schooling was a help or a hindrance in the development of religious awareness, whether through the influence of teachers, books, or general environment?

4. How far were you influenced, whether positively or negatively, by Church worship, or other forms of organized religion?

5. Do you think that the formation of your sense of right and wrong was entirely due to the teaching of your parents or others close to you? Or was there ever a sense of conflict between such a socially-induced "conscience" and any religious feelings of your own?

6. Can you recall any particular moment, or period, when you had a feeling of emerging into self-consciousness, that is of feeling yourself to be an individual person with some degree of freedom and responsibility? And was this associated with any religious feelings or ideas?

7. Can you remember when you first became aware of, or began thinking about, death, and what your early feelings about it were?

8. Some people look back to childhood experience as having been clearer, more vivid, more revealing than those of later life; while others see their early experiences as only the first steps in a process of growing awareness, which only came to full understanding in adulthood, or may not yet be complete. Do you feel that your experience falls into either of these two groups, or do you see some quite different pattern in your life?

9. Finally, how far can you really separate your early religious feelings or ideas from the interpretation you later put on them? It is of course very difficult, perhaps impossible, to recall what it really felt like to be a child, but perhaps one can do something to distinguish between the *feelings* one had as a child and the *meaning* one subsequently came to give them.

ANALYSIS OF REPLIES

Q. 1. How much do you think that you owe your early religious ideas or feelings to the influence of your family, or to any other individuals who were helpful, whether as models to be imitated or just as sympathetic people to talk to?

Table 1.

	F	M	All
A: Not at all	73 (26%)	29 (36%)	102 (28%)
B: To some extent	105 (37%)	20 (25%)	125 (35%)
C: Very much	104 (37%)	31 (39%)	135 (37%)
TOTALS	282	80	362

Analysis by Age-groups.

Table 2.

		F	M	All
— 35	A	10 (29%)	9 (50%)	19 (37%)
	B	16 (47%)	5 (28%)	21 (40%)
	C	8 (24%)	4 (22%)	12 (23%)
	TOTALS	34	18	52
36 — 59	A	33 (28%)	11 (39%)	44 (30%)
	B	42 (36%)	7 (25%)	49 (34%)
	C	43 (36%)	10 (36%)	53 (36%)
	TOTALS	118	28	146
60 +	A	24 (22%)	8 (27%)	32 (23%)
	B	37 (34%)	7 (23%)	44 (32%)
	C	48 (44%)	15 (50%)	63 (45%)
	TOTALS	109	30	139

Note: The ages of 25 respondents could not be established.

Q. 2. How far do you feel that your early idea of God was derived from what you saw in your parents?

Table 3.

	F	M	All
A: Not at all	199 (71%)	52 (65%)	251 (69%)
B: To some extent	47 (17%)	20 (25%)	67 (19%)
C: Very much	35 (12%)	8 (10%)	43 (12%)
— (No answer)	1	0	1
TOTALS	282	80	362

Analysis by Age-groups:

Table 4.

		F	M	All
— 35	A	22 (64%)	15 (83%)	37 (71%)
	B	6 (18%)	3 (17%)	9 (17%)
	C	6 (18%)	0	6 (12%)
	—	0	0	0
	TOTALS	34	18	52
36—59	A	87 (74%)	17 (61%)	104 (72%)
	B	16 (14%)	9 (32%)	25 (17%)
	C	14 (12%)	2 (7%)	16 (11%)
	—	1	0	1
	TOTALS	118	28	146
60 +	A	75 (69%)	17 (57%)	92 (66%)
	B	20 (18%)	7 (23%)	27 (20%)
	C	14 (13%)	6 (20%)	20 (14%)
	—	0	0	0
	TOTALS	109	30	139

Q. 3. How far do you feel that schooling was a help or a hindrance in the development of religious awareness, whether through the influence of teachers, books or general environment?

Table 5.

	F	M	All
A: Definitely a help	73 (26%)	11 (14%)	84 (21%)
B: If anything, a help	80 (28%)	24 (30%)	104 (29%)
C: Neither, or a little of both	86 (30%)	25 (32%)	111 (31%)
D: If anything, a hindrance	28 (10%)	10 (12%)	38 (11%)
E: Definitely a hindrance	15 (6%)	10 (12%)	25 (8%)
TOTALS	282	80	362

Analysis by Age-groups:

Table 6.

		F	M	All
—35	A	3 (9%)	0	3 (6%)
	B	9 (26%)	6 (33%)	15 (29%)
	C	8 (24%)	6 (33%)	14 (27%)
	D	11 (32%)	2 (11%)	13 (25%)
	E	3 (9%)	4 (22%)	7 (13%)
	TOTALS	34	18	52
36—59	A	33 (28%)	1 (4%)	34 (23%)
	B	32 (27%)	10 (35%)	42 (29%)
	C	37 (31%)	8 (28%)	45 (31%)
	D	10 (9%)	6 (22%)	16 (11%)
	E	6 (5%)	3 (11%)	9 (6%)
	TOTALS	118	28	146
60 +	A	32 (29%)	10 (33%)	42 (30%)
	B	34 (31%)	6 (20%)	40 (28%)
	C	34 (31%)	10 (33%)	44 (32%)
	D	3 (3%)	2 (7%)	5 (4%)
	E	6 (6%)	2 (7%)	8 (6%)
	TOTALS	109	30	139

Q. 4. How far were you influenced, whether positively or negatively, by church worship or other forms of organized religion?

Table 7.

	F	M	All
A: Quite positively	90 (32%)	22 (28%)	112 (31%)
B: If anything, positively	71 (25%)	19 (23%)	90 (25%)
C: Not at all, or a little each way	81 (28%)	26 (32%)	107 (30%)
D: If anything, negatively	27 (10%)	7 (9%)	34 (9%)
E: Quite negatively	13 (5%)	6 (8%)	19 (5%)
TOTALS	282	80	362

Analysis by Age-groups:

Table 8.

		F	M	All
—35	A	6 (18%)	5 (28%)	11 (21%)
	B'	7 (20%)	5 (28%)	12 (23%)
	C	11 (32%)	4 (22%)	15 (29%)
	D	4 (12%)	3 (16%)	7 (13%)
	E	6 (18%)	1 (6%)	7 (13%)
	TOTALS	34	18	52
36—59	A	38 (32%)	6 (21%)	44 (30%)
	B	36 (31%)	8 (29%)	44 (30%)
	C	29 (25%)	10 (36%)	39 (27%)
	D	11 (9%)	2 (7%)	13 (9%)
	E	4 (3%)	2 (7%)	6 (4%)
	TOTALS	118	28	146
60 +	A	41 (38%)	10 (33%)	51 (37%)
	B	23 (21%)	5 (17%)	28 (20%)
	C	34 (31%)	10 (33%)	44 (31%)
	D	9 (8%)	2 (7%)	11 (8%)
	E	2 (2%)	3 (10%)	5 (4%)
	TOTALS	109	30	139

Q. 5. Do you think that the formation of your sense of right and wrong was entirely due to the teaching of your parents or others close to you? Or was there ever a sense of conflict between such a socially-induced "conscience" and any religious feelings of your own?

Table 9.

	F	M	All
A: Sense of right and wrong entirely due to teaching	133 (48%)	48 (61%)	181 (51%)
B: Largely due to teaching, but some personal feeling	30 (11%)	1 (1%)	31 (8%)
C: Influence of teaching and personal feeling about equal	54 (20%)	9 (11%)	63 (18%)
D: Partly due to teaching but personal feeling dominant	36 (13%)	16 (20%)	52 (15%)
E: Wholly due to personal feeling	21 (8%)	5 (7%)	26 (8%)
— (no answer)	8	1	9
TOTALS	282	80	362

Q. 5. (cont.)

Analysis by age-groups:

Table 10.

		F	M	All
—35	A	14 (41%)	11 (61%)	25 (48%)
	B	7 (21%)	0	7 (13%)
	C	7 (21%)	3 (17%)	10 (19%)
	D	4 (11%)	4 (22%)	8 (16%)
	E	2 (6%)	0	2 (4%)
	—	0	0	0
	TOTALS	34	18	52
36—59	A	58 (51%)	13 (48%)	71 (50%)
	B	15 (13%)	1 (4%)	16 (11%)
	C	21 (18%)	4 (15%)	25 (17%)
	D	14 (12%)	5 (18%)	19 (14%)
	E	7 (6%)	4 (15%)	11 (8%)
	—	3	1	4
	TOTALS	118	28	146
60 +	A	53 (50%)	21 (70%)	74 (55%)
	B	5 (5%)	0	5 (4%)
	C	24 (23%)	2 (7%)	26 (19%)
	D	15 (14%)	6 (20%)	21 (15%)
	E	8 (8%)	1 (3%)	9 (7%)
	—	4	0	4
	TOTALS	109	30	139

Note: In this, as in the other tables, the percentages given are of those in each group that gave an answer.

Q. 6. Can you recall any particular moment or period when you had a feeling of emerging into self-consciousness, that is of feeling yourself to be an individual person with some degree of freedom and responsibility? And was this associated with any religious feelings or ideas?

A: experience associated with religious feelings or ideas
B: experience not thus associated
C: experience associated with rejection of religious ideas

Table 11.

Age at time of experience	F				M				All			
	A	B	C	Total	A	B	C	Total	A	B	C	Total
Under 1	1	0	0	1	0	0	0	0	1	0	0	1
1	1	2	0	3	0	0	0	0	1	2	0	3
2	0	3	0	3	0	0	0	0	0	3	0	3
3	2	2	0	4	0	1	0	1	2	3	0	5
4	1	3	0	4	1	1	0	2	2	4	0	6
5	3	3	0	6	3	2	0	5	6	5	0	11
6	8	6	0	14	0	4	0	4	8	10	0	18
7	3	4	0	7	0	2	0	2	3	6	0	9
8	1	5	1	7	2	1	0	3	3	6	1	10
9	5	3	0	8	0	1	1	2	5	4	1	10
10	5	6	0	11	1	0	0	1	6	6	0	12
11	4	2	0	6	0	3	0	3	4	5	0	9
12	6	4	0	10	0	0	2	2	6	4	2	12
13	6	5	0	11	2	0	0	2	8	5	0	13
14	5	2	1	8	2	0	0	2	7	2	1	10
15	3	3	0	6	2	1	1	4	5	4	1	10
16	2	1	1	4	1	0	0	1	3	1	1	5
17	3	2	0	5	0	1	0	1	3	3	0	6
18	3	0	0	3	0	1	0	1	3	1	0	4
19	1	0	0	1	0	0	0	0	1	0	0	1
20 and over	8	5	1	14	4	0	0	4	12	5	1	18
	71	61	4	136	18	18	4	40	89	79	8	176
No such experience recorded				146				40				186
TOTALS				282				80				362

Q. 7. Can you remember when you first became aware of, or began thinking about, death, and what your feelings about it were?

Table 12.

	F	M	All
A: Feelings of fear or disturbance	74 (26%)	17 (21%)	91 (25%)
B: Feelings of indifference, or no feelings recorded	112 (40%)	49 (61%)	161 (44%)
C: Feelings of assurance or welcome	74 (26%)	9 (11%)	83 (23%)
D: Feelings of awe, wonder or mystery predominant	13 (5%)	3 (4%)	16 (5%)
E: Feelings ambivalent, fear and assurance mixed or alternating	9 (3%)	2 (3%)	11 (3%)
TOTALS	282	80	362

Q. 8. Some people look back to childhood experiences as having been clearer, more vivid, more revealing than those of later life, while others see their early experiences as only the first steps in a process of growing awareness which only came to full understanding in adulthood, or may not yet be complete. Do you feel that your experience falls into either of these two groups, or do you see some quite different pattern in your life?

Table 13.

	F	M	All
A: Childhood experience significant, adult experience less so	35 (13%)	11 (14%)	46 (13%)
B: Childhood and adult experience of equal significance	50 (18%)	12 (15%)	62 (17%)
C: Childhood experience significant, adult experience more so	196 (69%)	56 (71%)	252 (70%)
— (No reply)	1	1	2
TOTALS	282	80	362

Analysis by age-groups:

Table 14.

		F	M	All
—35	A	1 (3%)	1 (6%)	2 (4%)
	B	3 (9%)	2 (11%)	5 (10%)
	C	30 (88%)	15 (83%)	45 (86%)
	—	0	0	0
	TOTALS	34	18	52
36—59	A	14 (12%)	5 (18%)	19 (13%)
	B	25 (22%)	4 (14%)	29 (20%)
	C	78 (66%)	19 (68%)	97 (67%)
	—	1	0	1
	TOTALS	118	28	146
60 +	A	14 (13%)	4 (14%)	18 (13%)
	B	18 (17%)	6 (21%)	24 (18%)
	C	77 (70%)	19 (65%)	96 (69%)
	—	0	1	1
	TOTALS	109	30	139

Q. 9. How far can you really separate your early religious feelings or ideas from the interpretation you later put on them? It is of course very difficult, perhaps impossible, to recall what it really felt like to be a child, but perhaps one can do something to distinguish between the *feelings* one had as a child and the *meaning* one subsequently came to give them.

A: Felt able to distinguish more or less clearly between childhood feelings and subsequent interpretation.

B: Felt a continuity or identity between childhood and subsequent experience making any such distinction difficult or impossible.

—: no answer attempted.

Table 15.

	F	M	All
A	159 (61%)	54 (69%)	213 (63%)
B	102 (39%)	24 (31%)	126 (37%)
—	21	2	23
TOTALS	282	80	362

Q. 9. (cont.)

Analysis by age-groups:

Table 16.

		F	M	All
—35	A	27 (89%)	15 (83%)	42 (84%)
	B	5 (16%)	3 (17%)	8 (16%)
	—	2	0	2
	TOTALS	34	18	52
36—59	A	64 (58%)	18 (64%)	82 (59%)
	B	47 (42%)	10 (36%)	57 (41%)
	—	7	0	7
	TOTALS	118	28	146
60+	A	59 (58%)	19 (66%)	78 (60%)
	B	42 (42%)	10 (34%)	52 (40%)
	—	8	1	9
	TOTALS	109	30	139

INDEX

John H. Westerhoff, III
Will Our Children Have Faith?
"A fine addition to the growing literature about the congregation as a central element in the Christian experience."
—Religious Education

"Sparkles with ideas, provokes arguments, conveys with clarity deep convictions." *—Theology Today*

Paperback   144pp